A

PRINCE OF WALES

LONG AGO:

A Bardic Legend of the Twelfth Century.

BY

LADY MARSHALL.

LONDON: WHITTAKER AND CO.,
PRICHARD, ROBERTS, AND CO., CHESTER.
1855.

To my Sister.

MY DEAR SISTER,

I cannot allow this work to be launched into life without a word of introduction to yourself, and a very few other kind friends who have taken a lively interest in its progress,—one of whom, in truth, suggested the idea,—and to whom I am really indebted for the encouragement which has carried me through with it; and I hereby record to you, and them, the cordial thanks and kindest wishes of

THE AUTHOR.

PEN-Y-CARDDEN,
    May, 1855.

PREFACE.

To restore to life, and to endue with that vitality which local traditions, with their local particularities, can alone afford. the most interesting event handed down to us through those channels peculiar to ourselves — the long silent strain of our Bards — is the object of the following tale.

That it shall fail in doing justice to a subject so well worthy of the genius of a SCOTT, and which may, by the similarity of its design, be brought into comparison with the minstrel tales of Scotland, is fully anticipated; but yet, a sentiment approaching to confidence is experienced that the subject is one which will appeal to the warmest sympathies of all who feel pride in the now general name of Briton.

There is no race, no language. now recognized

on the globe that has better claims, than the Welsh, to such respect as is due to authentic antiquity. Our language, the most pure of the various dialects of the Celtic, has yet such undoubted affinity to the Hebrew, and to others of the most known languages of the East, as to entitle us to claim the same affinity in point of race with the most celebrated nations of the ancient Eastern World; while there is no reason to doubt that, transplanted at some indefinitely remote period to our favoured soil,—to this island, this then remote spot of earth,—this "fortress built by nature for herself,"—the race were not long in displaying those qualities which developed equally, in the later immigrants to our soil.—the Saxon and the Norman races,—bid fair to subdue by their energy and to stamp with their own image of laws, institutions and manners, the various races of men who inhabit the earth.

This result, if such be the destiny of our country, is attributable, as its most obvious cause, to that particular manifestation of energy and independence of character which consists in braving the difficulties and the dangers attendant upon seeking a home in foreign and unknown lands; and it is to the first known step in this direction that the attention of the reader is called in the following poem.

Prince MADOG, a younger son of Owain Gwynedd, known to history as the successful defender of his country against the invasion of Henry II., left the shores of Wales, with a few companions, and established a Colony in some part of North America: he returned once, and having re-embarked with a reinforcement, was heard of no more, until by the researches of Catlin, the recent American traveller, traces of this colony were brought to light in the remarkable tribe of Mandans, on the banks of the Mississippi. The circumstances which led to the voluntary exile of this Prince form the staple of the narrative.

The period to which our historical legend relates is the middle of the Twelfth Century. The territory of Wales,—(CYMRU)—then independent of England, was divided into several states,—namely, Gwynedd, comprising part of what is now called North Wales; Powis, comprising other portions of it, and also wide districts of the neighbouring English Counties; and Gwent, or South Wales. With this last division we have nothing at present to do, as our scene does not touch upon that territory.

The tale itself is of sufficient interest to bear translation into prose; and my readers may perhaps entertain in its perusal some of the sentiments which first induced me to attempt clothing it in its original and natural language of poetry.

OWAIN GWYNEDD, one of the most valiant and patriotic of the Sovereign Princes of Cymru, being now well stricken in years, and still more worn by toil and battle than by age, bethought him of providing for the succession to his throne when he should be gathered to his fathers, and fixed upon his youngest son, MADOG, for that purpose, he being a prince of the greatest valour, wisdom, and gentleness, and endeared to the people by those qualities. MEURIG HÊN, a Prophet-bard, had predicted that he would ascend "the throne of the West," provided he was crowned during his father's life time on the nest-crag of an eagle.

Such prophecies often bring about their own completion; and this one, favouring, as it did, the views of sovereign and subjects, seemed about to work its fulfilment. But the oracle, like those of heathen times, had a double meaning, and "THE WEST," instead of being limited to Wales, the most westerly part of Britain, pointed still farther— namely, to AMERICA.

The inaugural ceremony was performed on the return of the prince from an expedition, wherein he had commanded the armies of Gwynedd, which had been sent by Owain to aid his ally and neighbour, Grüffydd, King of Powis, in expelling an invasion of his territories.

During his intercourse with the court of this prince, Madog had, unconsciously, made a conquest of another kind, namely, the monarch's only child and heir, Erffraid, a princess of surpassing beauty, but of strong passions and imperious will, while he himself was already secretly enamoured of a fair shepherdess, whose flocks he had saved from the onslaught of a pack of wolves, an adventure which he met with accidentally in one of his hunting expeditions. This shepherdess, whose name was Gwendda, was indeed descended from a former race of kings, but being reduced to a humble condition, dwelt with her mother, in the wilderness, and kept her flocks. On his return home, after his victorious campaign, he was received with acclamations in his own country, and preparations were instantly made for placing on his brows the insignia of successional royalty, which consisted of a band, or circle, of gold, without other ornament. At the same time every care was taken to fulfil the terms of the oracle, as delivered by the bard, and a fragment of rock from the heights of Snowdon, where the eagle had built, was brought down to the site of an ancient Carnedd, long deemed a spot of high sanctity, in the Vale of Corwen.

To this hallowed ground the prince was conducted in one continued ovation, for twenty miles, namely, from the frontier palace or castle, the seat of his habitual residence, where he guarded that, the most exposed flank of his father's dominions; and this forms the opening scene of the Poem.

On arriving at the sacred spot, the Prince was received by the whole of the dignities of Gwynedd except such as had accompanied his chariot, and at their head his royal Father and Grüffydd, King of Powis, with his daughter, the Princess Erffraid. Here, also, was the Prophet-Bard, filled with the inspirations of his genius, and ready to pour them forth in exultations at the progress of their fulfilment. But when, before the anointing of the Hereditary Prince, he proceeded to give utterance to his visions, he found that they came over his soul in a manner quite different from what he had intended. Instead of beholding Madog pursuing a long career of glory in peace and war, he saw him ploughing the ocean, and then vanishing from his eyes! Overcome with grief and disappointment, he disappeared from the scene, while the sensation caused by the arrival of the Prince, drew off the attention of the assemblage. The ceremony, however, damped for the moment by this ill omen, proceeded; and in their joy at seeing their young hero established as their future Sovereign, the people were partly consoled for the loss of even their prophet-bard. But misfortunes were not to end here. On descending from the altar where he had been crowned, the Prince was supported by the two Kings; and now came to light a project which they had, not unnaturally, formed, and which they judged the present the fittest occasion to announce, namely, that of uniting in marriage the sovereign elect of the one realm to the presumptive heiress of the other; the brave Prince of Gwynedd to the beautiful Princess of Powis. What was the grief and disappointment of those chiefs, when the Prince, in respectful but peremptory terms, declined the proposed alliance, without giving any reasons beyond the negative excuse of inability! • They were astounded at this turn of events, and their dismay was increased still further by the abrupt departure of the Princess, and which naturally drew after it that of her royal father; thus shaking the close alliance between the neighbour kings.

Nor was Madog himself unmoved by a state of things so painful to all parties. To disappoint the views of his father, to disregard the wishes of the nation, and to slight the feelings of a woman, though those feelings were now first made known to him, was a sore trial. Yet he swerved not for a moment from the path of honour. He would not degrade himself by sacrificing his own best affections, nor trifle with an affection which he had solicited, though danger and difficulty were the consequence of adhering to his purpose. Now, therefore, both to soothe his own mind after the scene he had gone through, and also, because his affairs had come to a crisis which he thought it due to the partner of his heart that she should be informed of, he repaired to the cot where the young shepherdess and her mother dwelt, and in an interview with the former first made himself known as Prince Madog.

This journey was unfortunate for Madog.— It prevented him from receiving, at his inauguration feast, the chiefs of the noble tribes of Gwynedd; a circumstance which was taken advantage of by his wily and ambitious brother,

UTHYR. This prince stood in a double rivalry to Madog, being not only one of his competitors in the succession, but also in the regards of the Princess of Powis. This opportunity, therefore, of Madog's absence from the feast, was made the most of by Uthyr: he craftily managed, in his own harangues, and also in the improvisations of a bard who was his creature, to foment the spirit of disaffection to Madog which he had long been secretly working up among a faction of the leading chiefs. The return of the Prince, ere the conclusion of the banquet, with the announcement that the King, who had been prevented from being present, through the shock caused by the termination of the inaugural ceremony, together with the abrupt departure of his royal guests, had become further indisposed, suddenly broke up the festivities, and threw a gloom over everything.

To deprecate these evil omens, according to the notions of those times, the aged monarch resolved to make a pilgrimage to all the holy places which lay in his route homeward to his royal residence at Aberffraw, in Anglesea. Uthyr obtained leave to go to Powis, and endeavour to conciliate the fair princess of that fair land; for, as among the various titles to succession, in those days, when that point was so unsettled, it was esteemed of great importance to be already wedded to a lady of sovereign, or at least of royal position, a marriage with Erffraid would be an additional prop to his pretensions, when at the death of Owain, which could not now be distant, the struggle should begin. There was like to be several competitors, should all who had a claim put it forward.

Iorwerth* was the eldest son; but eldership

* This Prince, during the turmoils into which his country fell after Madog's departure, took sanctuary at the shrine of St. Melangell, or Monacella, in a most secluded valley among the offsets of the Berwyn range; but passing bounds, he was seized on by his enemies and killed, and buried in the Church-yard of that picturesque solitude, "where," says a notice in the *Archæological Journal (Cambrensis)*, of April, 1848, "his coffin lid still exists, with this inscription,

HIC JACET EDWART."

But the author and a party of friends, since the above was written, paid a visit to the Church-yard in question, and there found, indeed, the tomb of Iorwerth, with the effigy of the princely sire of the Great Llywellin reposing thereon,— but on his shield, between the lions rampant was incised the name of "JOHN JONES"! and a date of eighteen hundred and something; and the tourists were informed that, in effect, Mr. J. J. (probably a topping farmer of the neighbourhood) died, and that Iorwerth's coffin lid had been lifted up, and the modern Celt been deposited beneath!

One of the tourists vented the feelings which boiled over on the occasion as follows —

      Most of us love posthumous fame,
      Grand coffins, an undying name;
        But, surely, never Death
      From any better met his match
      Than them on Iorwerth's shield who scratch
      A Jones,—and off his tombstone snatch,
        To lay a Jones beneath!

was then not all-conclusive; and he having a personal blemish, in the *shape* of a *shapeless* nose, was considered to be unfit for a Cymric crown, which might only encircle a brow favoured by nature; though in all other respects he was of a most princely conduct and attributes. Hywel was of a gay and chivalrous character, and Uthyr deemed that he would not be a formidable rival in political affairs.

This son attended his father on his pilgrimage; and while the King was gone to consult an oracle, at a shrine of an ancient saint, whose very name had been lost in the lapse of ages, but which on that account had acquired a stronger hold on the superstitious credulity of the people of every grade, the prince roamed through a secluded glen in the vicinity, and diverted his romantic

ANOTHER.

Poor Iorwerth sought to save his life,
In refuge from fraternal strife,
   At fair Melangell's shrine:
'T was vain,—the persecutors' hounds
Got scent of him when passing bounds,
   And made his head the fine.

Sure, never fate to any prince
Shewed such a grudge before or since,—
   No rest for skin or bones,—
All through his life-time he was *snubbed*,
And after death his grave is grubbed:
And, if his tombstone 's ever *rubbed*,
   He 'll pass for " *Mr. Jones* "!

fancy by singing to his harp. As he sung he seemed to hear a responsive strain of music, of an undefined and almost unearthly nature. In spite of the dangerous character of the place, or rather urged on by the difficulty of the enterprise, which he imagined might result in the deliverance of some captive damsel, he dashed from crag to crag, down to the dark abyss below, and there found,—not indeed an imprisoned lady, but a cavern made by the rushing torrent, and in it, leaning still upon his harp, which poured forth Æolic streams of sound—the Prophet-Bard,—dead. This cave had been one of the solitudes whither he used to resort in the times of his inspiration; hither he had wandered from the scene of his dismay; and here, unable to penetrate the mystery which had scared his spirit, his heart had broke, while still his hands clasped the harp, wont to reply to his every thought, but whose sounds he could no longer interpret.

To do funereal honours to the venerated "Delyniwr"* was now the impulse of the youthful prince, himself a bard of no mean grade; he hastened to join his father's train, and in the

* Harper.

gathering twilight groped his way towards the scene of their pilgrim duties.

It was a spot of extraordinary sanctity, indeed of holy, or rather superstitious awe : prophetic responses were, or were believed to be, given at the altar, under certain conditions of consultation. It was so contrived that, though it had three sides, only one of them could be approached without going round to a distance, each side being entered by a long cell or vault. Nor was it permitted for any suppliant to visit more than one of these cells, on pain of vitiating the response, and perhaps further penalties.

In the meantime Uthyr was on his embassy at the Powis Court, kept then at Trefaldwyn Castle, the modern Montgomery. He was at first received with scorn by the Princess; but on his making it appear that by wedding him she might defeat Madog of his succession, she listened to his advances, with the stipulation that he should find out and bring her the object of Madog's preference; that such an individual existed she made sure, being convinced that nothing but a prior attachment could make him or any man insensible to her charms. In vain did Uthyr, who was not so deeply impressed with that necessity, and, in truth, knew nothing of the state of his brother's affections, submit the somewhat exigeant nature of the Princess's command: she insisted, and instructed him to obtain the desired information by presenting himself on an early day, towards evening, at the shrine of a certain saint or divinity who was compelled to answer truly any question inscribed on his (or her) altar with *the blood of one born to inherit a throne*. At the same time she slightly punctured with a diamond-hilted dagger, which she wore in her girdle, her own delicate arm, and, catching the spouting fluid in a crystal phial, corked it up, and confided it to the Prince, giving him directions for his route, and then summarily dismissing him from her presence till the mission was fulfilled.

Uthyr departed on his errand in no very happy humour; he was somewhat, perhaps, of an *esprit fort* for those days; moreover, he had not been much flattered by the Princess's reception of him: and he thought her persecution of Madog's intended, even if such a person could be found, simply ridiculous. Indeed, his own views would have been to forward any such schemes, and get Madog fairly entangled with a plebeian wife, which would have been another prop to his own plans.

But he had been forced by the Princess's imperious will into the service; and away he rode across the Berwyn solitudes, with the precious phial in his valise.

As he drew near to the place where the oracular altar was situated, a thicket of ancient oak trees in the midst of a mountain wilderness, the thought struck him, that he was under no necessity of making any of the silly enquiries the Princess had ordered; and that he might put some question more interesting to himself with the infallible blood; and either tell her that the reply mentioned no lady as beloved of Madog, or else pick up some substitute by the way, and deliver her over to the Princess's mercy as the veritable *fiancée* of his brother.

Cheered at this new light, Uthyr groped into a compartment of the triangular souterrain, at the prescribed hour of dusk, dipped his finger into the royal blood, and wrote on the stone, *Shall Uthyr reign on Gwynedd's throne?* when a well-known voice from an adjoining cell, which he recognised as that of his father, was clearly audible, putting up a fervid prayer that Madog would not persist in throwing his crown away, and endangering the peace of his realm, by wedding beneath his rank; and at the conclusion of this impassioned address a voice was distinctly heard to answer—" Never ! "

This, taken as a reply to both his father's question and his own, staggered Uthyr, but pleased him not. He was, as we have said, not very impressible ; yet the prevailing superstitions of the age were not without their influence upon him. But he resolved, in spite of the interdict set upon such a proceeding, to explore the cell from which the oracle had spoken; for, as its reply had proved so far from satisfactory, he did not care for neutralising its efficacy. Moreover, if the voice should prove to come from a mere woman, instead of a Divinity, as he strongly suspected, she might serve his purpose as a victim for the Princess, and the representative for Madog's supposed bride. Accordingly, the Prince, after waiting to hear his father retire from the cell on one side, went round to that on the other side, and here he found, in effect, a young girl on her knees before the shrine.

She was alarmed at the sight of Uthyr, who, indeed, treated her with little ceremony, and was about to drag her roughly away, with the purpose above mentioned, when her cries brought another to her rescue, namely, Hywel, returning from his twilight adventures in the Glyn. Hedd, Uthyr's squire, also came to the spot, and Uthyr was obliged to relinquish his prize, whom they conducted to the tent of the royal cortège, camping not far distant for the night, and brought into the presence of the King, Uthyr accusing her of transgressing the canons of the Church by feigning to give oracular replies at the altar.

Thus accused, the damsel threw herself at the feet of the King, and entreated his mercy and forgiveness, at the same time announcing herself as Gwendda, the betrothed of his son Madog; confessing that she had uttered the reply in question, and renouncing for ever the dangerous yet dear distinction of becoming his wife; thus leaving him unfettered to fulfil his high destiny, and assure the welfare of his country.

Owain was touched by her charms and generosity, and would have sent her back to her mother with honour had not his confessor interposed, and urged the expediency of her retiring to a convent; an arrangement to which neither had the energy to object, and Gwendda disappeared from the scene as only the recluses of the Church do disappear, Madog himself, deeply as we may conclude that he lamented her loss, being powerless to snatch her from that living tomb, or indeed to trace what had become of her.

Uthyr contrived to make good his story to the fair Erffraid, and obtained her royal hand ere the crisis he was preparing for had arrived, namely, the death of his father. Owain died, full of years and glory, as the old story books say,—and in some things we cannot improve upon their phraseology,—he breathed out his great soul at Aberffraw, in Mona; and all the land was plunged into grief, Madog, his loving and most beloved son, being stunned by the blow as much as if he must not have been expecting it for years. Down the lovely Menai he conveyed the remains of the royal hero, in a state becoming them both, to lay them in the Minster at Bangor, founded by the holy Saint Dunawd, and the resting-place of many of the holy, the royal and the brave. For three days did Madog, attended by the Notables of Gwynedd, keep watch and ward over these precious relics, with every ray of daylight excluded from the vast choir, which yet rivalled day itself in the brightness of its waxen and perfumed torches.

At length the moment came when the devoted son must bid an everlasting adieu to the earthly tenement which had held the best of fathers; must look, for the last time, on his noble and beloved face. Then was it customary for the Sovereign accessant of Gwynedd to take the crown from the head of the royal corpse, give it to a bishop who stood at hand prepared to receive it, lift the golden bandlet from his own head, and receive instead, from the bishop, the crown which he had just placed in his hands. Madog was now in the midst of these accustomed ceremonials. He had reverently taken the crown from the venerated head that had so long worn it to his own glory and that of his country; he had lifted from his own head the badge of secondary rule, which he had also worn in the same manner; the bishop was about to encircle his brows, when the lid of the late King's coffin would have been shut, and the view of that loved face been for ever hid—a moment Madog lingered—in one more he would have been King of Gwynedd. But ere that moment arrived a clamour was heard outside, and soon also inside the Cathedral, shouts, and clarions, and echoes of war. The bishop dropped the crown, and the Prince sprang forward to learn the cause of the interruption. Need it be told? Uthyr and Erffraid, taking advantage of the period of mourning for the king, during which the country was of necessity less strictly guarded, had come by forced marches from Powis, and were now beleaguring the Minster, in which were shut up the chief strength of the state, and also some treacherous partisans of their own.

Madog, whose chief anxiety at this moment was for the precious relics of his sire, still lying exposed in their coffin, rushed up to the battlements to hold a parley with the invaders. They carried on the form long enough for their scheme, and then Madog, to his dismay, heard the heavy door grate upon its hinges, and the treacherous brother, vindictive woman, and their followers, pour into the spacious nave, where their adherents, who were mingled at chance among the other assistants at the funeral solemnities, everywhere began to play their part, so that confusion reigned throughout the crowd, none, scarcely, knowing friend from foe. Through this scene had Madog to make his way from the battlements to the high altar, a work of peril which was increased by the circumstance of his being entirely unarmed, any weapon being considered as a violation of the proprieties of royal and filial mourning weeds. But the thoughts of his father's remains being exposed to insult, far more than the crown which lay in jeopardy near them, gave an additional spur, if it were possible, to his valour; guarded by his faithful Rhirid, the brother of his Gwendda, he dashed through the fiend-like tumult that now filled every corner of the sacred edifice. But Uthyr and Erffraid, conducted by Ithel, the traitor Lord of Iäl, were within a few paces of the altar railing. In another moment they would have surmounted that barrier, though it was guarded by Prince Iorwerth himself. There was but one chance, one possibility of cutting off this movement. A lofty monument, erected to the memory of Grüffydd ab Cynan, Owain's father and predecessor, stood out at the angle of the choir, of precipitous height and form, but presenting some points to which an undaunted adventurer might cling,—Madog hesitated not, — from the shoulder of his attendant, Rhirid, he made a spring, clomb with unflinching energy over the figured blocks of marble that composed the gigantic grouping, and dropping, as a supernatural apparition from the point of an angel's wing, stood by the open coffin, just as Uthyr who had attained the same object from the opposite side, was about to stride across it and seize the prostrate crown.

Thus opposed, and somewhat abashed, the

usurper drew back; and, at the instant, the Princess, who was close on his track, drew her poniard and sprung forward to plunge it into Madog's unguarded breast, when, from the crowd which surrounded the centre group, a nun threw herself between the weapon and its destined object, and fell upon the open coffin at Madog's feet,—it was *his Gwendda!* She expired in his embrace; and, no longer feeling any taste for the common ambitions of the world, he at once announced his resignation of the crown, which he placed upon the head of Iorwerth's youthful son, LLYWELYN, afterwards called the Great; reserving to himself no further share in public affairs than to strengthen the young sovereign's reign.

Here ends the "Story"— properly so called. The invaders, staggered at the tragic scene, and at its results, withdrew their pretensions for the time: but a general state of disorder was soon renewed by the ambitious struggles of the sons of Owain, chiefly stirred up by Uthyr, so that Madog at length withdrew from the scene altogether, and sought to give a new direction to the energies of his countrymen, by heading an expedition for "the Conquest of Seas," as Mrs. Hemans appropriately terms it.

He sailed for "The West," and landed on the shores of the New World, where, it is not to be doubted, that he did much to advance the condition of the people whom he fell in with.

Thus was the voice of the oracle verified — he was

"THRONED IN THE WEST!"

A PRINCE OF WALES
LONG AGO.

CANIAD FIRST.

A PRINCE OF WALES LONG AGO.

CANIAD I.

LAND of the torrent, the lake, and the mountain,
   Land of the echo, the harp, and the song!
Why are no voices resistless recounting
   The charms and the triumphs to thee that belong?

Land of true hearts, noble thoughts, and kind feeling,
   Land of the lovely, the brave, and the free!
Why are not tongues in sweet harmonies pealing
   Their duty, their love, and their homage to thee?

Behold our fair Sister-lands radiantly glancing
   Approval on duteous children whose lays,
The glories of art and of nature enhancing,
   From ocean to ocean resound with their praise.

Sweet Scotia is lovely, or laughing, or frowning,
   But who can her beautiful features explore,
And study her various charms, without owning
   That she owes much to Nature—to Poetry more?

And thus pale Ierne—though often the breathing
  Her genius utters is tuned to her woes—
The spirit of song her wild deserts enwreathing,
  Makes them smile like the garden and bloom like
      the rose.

Then oh! for a voice loud and deep as the thunder,
  And soft as the rills through our vallies that run—
A pencil to dip in the colours that under
  The firmament blaze at the set of the sun!

Ah! was there but a minstrel old,
  To sing of castle, hold, and tow'r—
Of ladies fair, and barons bold,
  Like him of Yarrow's bow'r!

  Oft in the mysterious hour
  Of our sleep's relaxing power,
  When, beneath the blushing sky,
  Morning's welcome dawn is nigh,
  Visions undefined, but bright,
  Seem to dance upon the sight.

  Faces such as now we see,
  But in costume differing far;
    Sights and sounds that come and flee,
  Swell of music—crash of war—

Broken accents, such as lovers
Whisper in the summer shade,
 What time the deepening twilight covers
Blushes of the timorous maid.

Range yourselves, ye fleeting fancies;
Take a form, a hue, a plan;
 Weave, ye winged thoughts, the chances
Happening to some god-like man.

Now one by one, as if at the command
Of some invisible magician's wand.
Condensed from the surrounding air, they on the canvas stand.

The ground-work of the living picture seemed
The skirting of a mountain land; there streamed
A rocky river, serpentining round
The foot of many a fair projecting mound;
The off-sets of a range retreating high,
Whose farther ridges mingled with the sky;
In the mid distance, one embattled cone
Stood forth to guard the pass, majestic and alone.
Nearer, and where the mountain's sterner steep
Was softened to a verdant champaign sweep,
A wondrous rampart, earth-built, stretched away,
Marking the boundaries of rival sway—

Saxon and Celt—of rapine, war, and feud,
The watchwords then—now merged in brotherhood.
Some furlongs off there rose another wall;
Between, a neutral ground, was free to all.

Within the Celtic line, some bow-shot length,
A structure stood,[1] which, part for warlike strength,
And part for princely grandeur, seemed designed,
The palace and the fortalice combined:
Without were bastion, fosse and armed towers;
Within were ample halls, and stately corridores:
Of massive mould, adorned with simple skill,
Such as a rugged age's wants fulfil,
On every turret, arch, and " 'vantage coign,"
Emblem and badge of Gwynedd's royal line,
On banner blazon'd, and on stone impress'd,
Stood forth, in rampant rage, the Griffin Crest.

   And now that haughty symbol,
   With trumpet loud, and timbal,
   And harp's inspiring thrills
   Re-echoed from the hills,
Triumphant through the valley sweeps along:
   His worth and glory voicing,
   Ten thousand tongues rejoicing,

[1] Plas Madoc.

Give a youthful hero's name to song.
   Age, with tottering step, advancing,
   Steel-clad knights on war-steeds prancing,
   Female forms with bright eyes glancing,
Still the joyous notes prolong.

 "Hail! to our young defender,
   MADOG of the eagle eye!
 Our praise to him we render,
   Let it soar from earth to sky.
 His path is like the lightning,
   The mountain pine his form,
 His face like heaven brightening
   When clears the summer storm.

"Woe to the fierce invader
   Who treads our country's shores!
 Like a whirlwind down to aid her,
   His arrowy tempest pours.
 From the river to the ocean,
   From the Severn to the sea,
 Let hearts, with one emotion,
   Send forth their praise to thee!

"Chiefly, ye men of Powis,
   Maids and matrons, lift your hands

To the youthful chief, whose prowess
    Scattered wide your foemen's bands.
Iorwerth is a host in battle;
    Uthyr is a dragon's whelp;
When the iron hailstorms rattle,
    Hywel is a present help.

" But in hid or open danger,
    In the council, in the field,
MADOG MAELOR, The Avenger,
    He's our seer, our sword, our shield!"

So pealed the chorus on—but ere its close
    The measured chime was lost,
    For o'er th' enraptured host
The idol of their hero-worship rose.
    Upon his shield he stands,
    Uplifted by the hands
    Of those resistless bands
Who in the battle scattered death around.
    Now, with barbaric joy,
    They greet their chieftain boy;
The hills, the vales, the woods, the skies resound.

    Upon his downy face
    Scarce manhood 'gan efface

The stripling's softer grace ;
His limbs elastic were as willow wand;
　　Like him who, with a sling,
　　The giant's pride could bring
　　To nought, He seemed a thing
Unfitted savage war-men to withstand.

Yet, in his aspect, there was that which tells
　Of high command by gracious wisdom held ;
Of lofty purpose in the breast that dwells,
　But slumbers till by lofty call impell'd.

Nor in his triumph did his eye display
　A thought of vulgar glory, but the sense
Of solemn duty power must ever lay
　On those whom duty own—profound, intense !

Thus self-possessed, throughout that stirring day,
　He bore himself : the deafening tumult, first,
Of popular acclaim, which all the way
　His journey led, in growing transport burst ;

And deeper trial then—the joy to view
　Of tender kindred—an exulting sire ;
And him, that brave ally, whose crown was due,
　And nation's freedom, to his warlike fire.

They skirted far the rocky course[2]
Of that dark flood who at his source,
With all a full-grown giant's force,
    Springs forth from Tegid's womb.
Saluted from the warlike post
On Dinäs'[3] heights, their breasts they crossed,
Propitiatory to the ghost,
    At great ELISEG's[4] tomb;
Ere two descending torrents join,
Where winding vales their meads combine,
They followed Alwyn's verdant line,
    And left Dee's sounding shore.
At length, upon a swelling mound
Which gently rising hills surround,
They rested, and the sacred ground
    Was thenceforth called MAES-MAWR.[5]

There, upon such a throne
As Nature calls her own.

---

[2] The River Dee comes out of the lake commonly called Bala Pool, but properly Llyn Tegid, from a British king drowned in it by his enemies.

[3] Castell Dinäs Bran, the picturesque British Fort, overhanging the town of Llangollen and adding so much to the effect of its scenery, but of whose history, unhappily, no traces can be found by any researches.

[4] Eliseg, a British Chief, was slain in battle here, and a monumental cross erected to his memory by his great grandson Cyngen: 7th century.

[5] Now the seat of Mrs Manners Kerr; in the grounds are the remains of this remarkable carnedd.

The hand of man had piled
An altar vast and wild,—
Unshaped fragments, tempest-hurled
    From the eagle's realm on high,
When the eddying mists are whirled
    By winds that answer to his cry.

MEURIG HÊN.[6] the prophet-bard,
    This mysterious decree
In his desert vigils heard,
    Looking towards the utmost sea—

"*He who on an eagle's nest*
    With a circlet ye invest
    Shall be throned in THE WEST."

This oracle the people's voice
Points to the chieftain of their choice,
And its dark meaning to fulfil
Works their indomitable will.
Small effort was it then to drag
O'er hill and dale the ponderous crag;
From Snowdon's peak to Corwen's plain,
It scarcely seemed a finger's strain:

[6] An imaginary character; but the influence attributed to his bardic functions not so.

So well we bring about our ends.
When passion's force the purpose bends.

Now in the carnedd's centre stood
The stone from whence the royal brood
First stretched their spreading wings to try
Their glorious mission to the sky—
First fixed their steady gaze upon
The effulgence of the mid-day sun.

All this was present to the mind
Of him, that prophet, old and blind :
Nor did he fail to point its sense
With all that fervid eloquence
Which, in a rude and simple age,
Supplies the place of statutes sage ;
A code of laws devoid of art,
Unwritten, but upon the heart.

He shewed them how the silent stream
    Of time—events—achievements won,
Interpreted his desert dream,
    And centred all in Owain's son,
The latest born,[7] but yet most meet

---

[7] We here take our bardic privilege of *adapting* not *copying* history, and, without any scruple, *dock* Owain Gwynedd of thirteen sons at one blow. He had, historically speaking, eighteen sons, two threes by two wives, and twelve illegitimates, our hero being one of that number.

To sit upon his father's seat.
MADOG, supreme in peace or wars,
Among his brethren, star of stars!

The solemn scene is now prepared,—
Perhaps the heathen slightly shared
With rites more Catholic,—the wreath
Of mistletoe, with incense breath:
Alas, what boots it, since the twain
Are now alike accounted vain?

Bishops and Mitred Abbots proud,
Sprinkled with blessed drops the crowd;
Who yet, before those holy men,
Gave ear and eye to Meurig Hên,
As seated in a hollow oak,
Made sacred by the thunder-stroke,
With trembling hand, but touch of fire,
He swept his harp's prophetic wire.
Keenly his bright but sightless orbs.
 Seem to pierce pervading space,
While the vast *UNSEEN* absorbs
 His soul, and deepens o'er his face.

" In the lordly eagle's nest,
  Not the oldest, but the best

Hath dominion o'er the rest:
This is nature's law, impress'd,
Also, on the human breast.
Bow we to the Griffin crest,
And to Madog's high behest.

" Lo, I see him! Lo, I hear him!
  All a people's blessings cheer him ;
  Guardian angels hover near him—
    Spirits of his mighty race!

" But what is this obscures the glass
  On which unbidden visions pass
    Before the prophet's face?

" Is it that Madog's chariot wheels
  The dust of battle-fields conceals?
  Gliding on, he keeps his way,
  Sportive dolphins round him play;
  Not in dust, but ocean's spray,
  Slow the vision melts away—

" What can mean the strange portent?
  Are—are—the prophet's powers spent?"

The sound is gone, but still the eye,
  The sightless eye, is upward turned,

As it would burst ere not descry
   All in the labouring soul that burned.

Assembled thousands, breathless share
   The anguish of the bard's suspense,
And supplicate him to declare
   That wild out-pouring's hidden sense.

But not a sound appeared to reach
   The prophet's deafened ear;
His lips were moving, but his speech
   Was not for man to hear.

 And now the sprightly clang
 Of martial music rang
   Upon the answering air:
 Forgotten every pang,
 A shout exulting sprang—
"Welcome to Madog—Owain Gwynedd's heir!"

Hard were it to describe in words, I ween,
The progress of that wild and wondrous scene:
How tell of savage pomp—of ritual strange,
Beyond romantic fancy's widest range?
But howsoever rude their manners strike
Our judgment, nature is in all alike;

And though in modes and customs differing far,
Our fathers they, and we their children are.

The youthful victor gracefully receives
His rapturous welcome, and his chariot leaves;
Through widening throngs the escort passes on.
To where the royal sire awaits the son.
There, on a rustic dais, some steps above
The level lifted of the temple grove,
The aged monarch sat, while grouped around.
Fair dames and noble chiefs, his court, are found,
And by his side, in equal regal state,
Grüffydd,[8] the king of rescued Powis. sate,
Companioned by his only child and heir,
The beauteous Erffraid, boast of British fair:
On such a fragile scion hangs his hope,
While Gwynedd's rests upon a goodly troop
Of valiant princes, fitted to maintain
The glory and the triumphs of his reign.

This reign was now approaching to its close
By nature's law, and it was time he chose

---

[8] The nearest historic personage with whom I can identify this King is Grüffydd Maelor, mentioned in the Enwogion of Mr. Williams. He was only a co-king of Powis, which, like the other states of Cymru, often altered its limits. He had, instead of one daughter, one son. His wife, Angharad, was a daughter of Owain. "He exceeded in wisdom and liberality all the princes of his time," says Mr. Williams. Died 1109, and buried at Meivod.

A fit successor which th' accepted use
Of ancient times permitted him to choose,
His own, establishing the general voice,
The elders passed, on Madog fell the choice.
The father's office then it was to set
Upon the prince's brows the annulet—
A simple band of gold, devoid of gem,
Inferior to the regal diadem:
A crown successional; and this to wear
Was held to constitute the monarch's heir.

This usage, by long ages consecrate,
This time was honoured with unwonted state:
The recent triumphs of the aspirant king
With added speed the glorious crisis bring,
Which nations call for and which prophets sing.
The presence of an old and strict ally,
And lastly, but not least, the prophecy—
All shed an halo, more than rainbow bright,
Of hope and glory on the coming rite.

And when the sire, with age's feeble gait,
But spirit high, that age could not abate,
Stood by the kneeling figure of the son,
In act to place the glittering circlet on,

And raised for that the warrior's vizored casque,
And gave to view his face. 'twere hard to ask
A group more fitted for the Phidian task;
Or whether was the fairest sight, to say,
The dawn of manhood, or its setting ray.

One look, indeed, among the thousand fixed
Upon the picture, seemed as though there mixed
No balanced feeling in its earnest gaze,
But warm preferment of the opening rays.

 Who will not guess that this was she
  Who, 'spite of royal pride
 And maiden fear, had eyes to see,
  But had not art to hide—
The peerless fair of distant Severn side?

 And there was yet a sterner eye,
  Whose look malevolent,
 Upon the centre group on high,
  And on the look intent
The princess gave, was darkly, fiercely bent.

 Love and envy's double smart—
  A birthright lost, a passion scorned—
 Were foully festering in the heart,

And every joy to venom turned—
'Twas Uthyr with this fire that inly burned.

His royal father's hands uplift,
   Invoking heaven to shower down
On Madog's head its choicest gift,
   His country's welfare and his own,
Was gall and wormwood to the soul bereft
   Of heavenly seed, and all with weeds o'ergrown.

Oh, marvel 'tis how one whose life
   In childhood with another passed
Can afterwards, in savage strife,
   The gentle memories from him cast
   Of young companionship—what then can last?

'Tis marvel how the hands that wont to clasp,
   In sleep or play, another's neck around,
Can afterwards the cruel weapon grasp,
   The breast oft played or slept upon, to wound!
   Ah me, that foes in brothers can be found!

'Twas needful Uthyr should disguise
   The angry tumult of his soul;
And he was as a serpent wise,
   And hottest passions could control,
   With semblance cold and silent as the pole.

Soon he chased the darkling cloud
   From off his brow, and with a feint,
Joined in the acclamations loud,
   Which, when the circlet fair was bent
   Around the fairer head, the azure concave rent.

And then a pause—like sculptured stone,
   Or spell-bound as by magic wand,
There bends the father, kneels the son,
   And round the hundred thousands stand ;
   But soon 'tis past—the monarch lifts his hand.

And thus his accents flow :
   "Seasons come and go—
   Summer's heat and winter's snow—
And spring returns, though slow ;
   But man can never know
   A second spring,—his functions cease.
   Bless Thou the aged, GOD OF PEACE !

"The cedar's sap is dried,
   To the winds its glories flung,
But from its withered side
   A verdant shoot hath sprung—
Great GOD OF BATTLES, bless Thou the young !"

Such was the simple prayer
The aged man preferred—
  Oh, might it be accepted where
The heart is all, and nought the word!
Prayer, oft ungranted, never is unheard.

The silence of the awe-struck crowd
  Now into loud expression broke,
And acclamations deep and loud,
  The wide-felt exultation spoke:

Scarce intermitting to allow
  Space for the orthodox routine—
The choral chaunt—the unctuous flow—
  With censer's perfumed toss between.

Nor wholly satisfied until
  That priest who most their hearts desire
The bardic office should fulfil,
  And wake to song the hallowed lyre.

With Meurig's name the air is filled,
  And every deep and glen around:
But soon in sad amazement stilled—
  The prophet-bard can not be found!

In vain they search the leafy dell,
    The blasted tree—the caverned stone—
Nor eye could see, nor tongue could tell,
    Or how, or where the bard had gone.

Aghast with horror and with dread—
    An omen dire—a loved one lost—
A gloom desponding overspread,
    With baleful wing, the gathered host.

But quick succeeding joy and grief
    Alternate in the changeful mood
Of thronging numbers; both are brief,
    And passing as the summer cloud.

The ceremonial all complete,
    It was a touching sight to see
That multitude at Madog's feet,
    In loving homage, bend the knee—
'Twas like a gentle breeze rippling the summer sea.

Now risen from his knees he sate
    Erect upon the Eagle-stone,
Exalting in his regal state,
    And not exalted by a throne;
For bright in Madog all the princely graces shone.

The while, with aspect thus benign,
  The people's vows and prayers he met,
His inmost thoughts could not divine
  What trials waited on him yet ;
Alas, his onward way was all with thorns beset.

To render his descent more dignified,
A king supported him on either side ;
When midway, pausing, as with deep intent,
In conference low they each to other bent ;
And as resulting from their thoughts combined,
The royal Owain opened thus his mind :

"Thus, before heaven, and with the full accord
Of these our subjects, I, their sovereign lord,
In presence of our old and dear ally,
Our well-beloved son do dignify,
Invest, and clothe with all that doth pertain
To kingly grandeur, power, and domain.
The people's freedom, and the regal state
That is and will be, we consolidate ;
For British monarch ne'er yet stooped, nor shall,
To hold dominion over dastard thrall !
But this, our act and theirs, seems incomplete—
Man pines alone on e'en a royal seat—

And for the future, or for ours or theirs,
No surety can there be with lack of heirs :
This anxious thought the King of Powis shares.
The slender stem on which his hopes depend
Seems one which Zephyr's breath might almost bend;
And, like the pale and graceful eglantine,
Around some guardian oak should gently twine.
This double difficulty then suggests
Its obvious remedy, and all that rests
Is to unite the valiant and the fair,
And hearts and kingdoms by one act to pair :
Our brother king with every wish complies.
The fair one blushes—and what blush denies ?"

And she *did* blush, that haughty fair, and smile,
With eye averted, but with ear the while,
Expectant of the rapturous prompt reply,
Befitting lover fond to princess high.

But how is this ?—no voice she hears—she sees,
With side-long glance, no lover at her knees ;
With parted lip she lists, and stifled breath—
That moment seemed an age—that silence—death.
'Tis past—her dark suspense is scattered soon
By what makes e'en suspense itself a boon,

For she had rather been for ever there
Transfixed, than heard what she was doomed to hear.
Upon that minute's age-long silence broke
A low, clear, earnest voice; and Madog spoke:

"My liege and father, and our neighbour king,
Forgive your servant in this only thing—
My vital energies, my living powers—
The brain to think—the arm to act—are yours :
Whatever I, as subject and as son,
Can, is, when said by you, already done;
But there is one reserve, in man—one part
With which another meddleth not—the heart.
A subtle fire contains, and this to quench,
To mar his being is—his nature wrench :
And he's unworthy of the manly name
Who smothers or perverts this sacred flame.
Should then the Princess even condescend
In filial deference her will to bend.
A partner in the act I could not be—
Still free myself, let her be also free."

Oh, night is black, and blacker still the night
That follows the volcano's flashing light.
But what is nature's night—her wildest storm—
To passions that the human soul deform?

The Princess raised her head : a face more fair
Was never breathed upon by summer air ;
Each feature measured in the strictest line ;
A skin, as ripening peaches, soft and fine :
But over all a darkling shadow spread,
Like thunder drops upon a lily shed,
That blacker show upon so fair a head.
From 'neath a brow, in faultless moulding cast,
Her eyes of lucid radiance seemed to blast—
She rose, and noiseless, like a meteor, passed !

The effect may not be written, scarce be thought,
This passage on the scared beholders wrought :
So sudden and so silent was the change.
It seemed of something more than earthly strange.
The King of Gwynedd and the Powis Chief
Were with amazement staggered, and with grief.
The last, in haste, attended, as was meet
A father should, upon his child's retreat.
While, troubled all the high and courtly train,
In courtly bounds, surprise could scarce contain.
Among their groups, intently Uthyr eyed
The scene, with joy that scantly he could hide.
The impress made among the distant throng
Was all of something undefined, but wrong.

A PRINCE OF WALES
LONG AGO.

CANIAD SECOND.

CANIAD II.

AMONG the consolations given
To man, when grief and passion riven,
Although at first we scarcely feel
Its gentle influence o'er us steal,
The mute creation hath a power
Of soothing in the anguished hour.

The earth, the herb, the moving sky—
The beasts that roam, the birds that fly—
All speak a language, soft and kind,
To calm the sorrow-stricken mind.
The fevered, from their couch of pain,
Through the dim glass their eye-balls strain—
A fleeting cloud, a quivering bough,
Bring their relief, we know not how.
The prisoned wretch,[9] whose twilight cell
His steps hath echoed as they fell,
Till time he could no longer tell,
Hath, with the loathful thing that crawls,
Made friendship, on his dungeon walls.

A fit transition, then, it is, I deem,
From Maesmor's troubled mount to Alwen's stream:

[9] Related of a prisoner in the Bastile.

He in his ever varied course,
Had mythic fancies still their force,
One night imagine, as he winds,
Moved by antagonistic minds :
Now by a scourging demon driven,
Through gorges by his fury riven,
He foams in deeps that shut out heaven
Anon, as through the influence mild
Of some good fay, his frenzy wild
Is checked, and, murmuring soft, he spreads
His sleepy limbs o'er mossy meads.
But from his desert cradle, where
He steals from out the bosom fair
Of his Lake-Mother,[10] to the plain
That breaks the Berwyn barrier chain,
Where, joined in one with mighty Dee,
He rolls his volumes towards the sea,
No goodlier face he shows than when
He laves that osier-skirted glen
In which, retired from vulgar ken,
The Giant-king, in days of eld,
Like him of Cures, converse held
With one esteemed of higher mould
Than e'en earth's fairest. Thus we 're told
Of that deep vale that laps the feet
Of royal Dünmael's[11] lofty seat.

---

[10] The river Alwen flows out of a lake of that name, near Llanrwst, and into the Dee in the vale of Edernion.
[11] Gader Dünmael, a lofty mountain, overhanging the Alwen.

In confirmation of the tale,
We call it Contemplation's Vale.[12]

There, on a tufted steep,
   Where o'er the living rock,
Short, juicy grasses creep,
   At evening roamed the flock.

Their guardian was a maid
   Some twenty summers old,
And when the kidlings strayed
   Too widely from the fold,

She left her daisied seat,
   Let fall her flaxen thread,
Pursued with fairy feet,
   And home the stragglers led.

But yet it ofttimes happed
   Her distaff idle lay,
And, all in musings rapt,
   She let the kidlings stray.

What can it be that keeps
   Down-fixed the damsel's eyes?

---

[12] Llanfihangel Glyn Myfyr, on the Glen of Contemplation, at the foot of "Gader." See note preceding.

Her youthful face that steeps
  In deep suffusive dyes?

There stood a straw-roofed cot,
  Nooked in the narrow dell,
Wherein her humble lot
  Decreed the girl to dwell.

Roused by the warning bleat
  Of parted kid and dam,
From out the dim retreat
  An elder matron came.

The venial error's cause
  She gathered with a look,
Not such as overawes,
  But one of mild rebuke.

"Ah, say, my Gwendda, why,
  Thy distaff plying near,
Thy helpless charge's cry
  Dost thou unheeding hear?

" This day the pastoral care
  Is thine, and thine alone;
Thou saidst thy brother's share
  By thee should all be done.

" Thou know'st our grisly foes
    In watchful ambush lurk,
And none the moment knows
    When they may do their work :

"And though the onslaught late
    That on our flock they made
Was, by a happy fate,
    Upon their heads repaid,

" It may not chance that, when
    They make their next attack,
The Hunter of the Glen
    Will be upon their track,

" Who, with his hunting spear,
    Such havoc dealt around,
That in the coverts near
    No wolf for long was found.

" But, Gwendda, tell me true—
    When I that hunter name,
Why does thy lily hue
    All crimson into flame?

" I had a secret dread,
    And therefore did I speak

That name; and, ah, the red
   Is tell-tale in thy cheek!

"Alas, beware, my child—
   My simple mountain maid—
By handsome hunters wild
   Are damsels oft betrayed!

" His air, his dress, his speech,
   Though tuned to courtesy,
The merest hind may teach
   How lofty his degree.

"And though a royal name,
   From ancient Kings, we boast,
In poverty and shame
   The title long is lost."

The conscious maid could not
   Her mother's charge deny,
Nor say, in language, what
   Was gainsaid in her eye.

But lifting up, at length,
   Like drooping flower, her head,
With woman's gentle strength,
   She to her mother said :

"Oh, pardon, mother dear,
    Load, load thy child with blame,
But, blessed mother, spare
    The generous Hunter's name.

"For us he risked his life :
    Ah me, I see it still,
The long and bloody strife—
    It makes my heart turn chill !

"Alone he met the pack,
    Through numbers waxing bold,
Down, down from each attack
    A gnashing monster rolled !

" Oh, 'twas a wondrous thing—
    It was a god-like mein—
As if the Giant King
    Again on earth were seen !

"And could it ever be,
    That one so kind and brave
Could mean to injure me
    His arm was stretched to save ?

" Of every vain alarm,
    Oh chase away the thought ;

With nothing kin to harm
    Can such a man be fraught!"

The mother shook her head,
    And smiled a mother's smile;
"Guileless thyself." she said.
    "Thou dreamest not of guile :

"Nor I myself, except
    The mysteries that surround
Our guest, could e'er suspect,
    From such a hand, a wound.

"I marvel there has passed
    An interval so long
Since he has hunted last
    These solitudes among ;

"It may be that engaged
    The youth hath been in war,
Which, rumour says, hath raged
    Upon the frontier far ;

"Or, it may be—but hush—
    My child, I'll say no more.
Ah me, in torrents gush
    Thy tears my bosom o'er !

"When Rhirid shall return
　　From Madog's festal show,
My Gwendda, we shall learn
　　If all these things be so."

'Twas as she said, fair Gwendda hiding
Her blushes at her mother's chiding,
　　And, ah, still more, the fear
Her mother's broken words suggested,
Her head upon her shoulder rested
　　And loosed the struggling tear.

Too true—their young unknown defender,
The brave, the kind, and, ah, the tender,
　　Who all her spirit swayed,
In savage strife he might have perished,
Or she, her love no longer cherished,
　　Herself be worse than dead.

Man, with the stir of life surrounded,
The stingings of a spirit wounded
　　May smile at, or forget;
But when a woman's love is slighted,
Her being is for ever blighted,
　　Her sun for ever set.

See the gay bark from harbour starting,
Through sparkling waves like dolphin darting,
   Of hope the image fair,
When treacherous hidden rocks have cleft her,
And on the waste of waters left her,
   The emblem of despair!

And this lone, melancholy beacon,
By help—by hope—by all forsaken,
   Is yet far less forlorn
Than woman's heart when once expanded
And then on disappointment stranded,
   A bye-word and a scorn.

Full many an eye that sparkled brightly,
Full many a step that tripped it lightly,
   When love was first a guest;
Too soon the despot's rule obeying,
The altered look and gait betraying,
   Bespeak the heart oppressed.

And this fair Gwendda's cheek was blenching,
And this her eye's soft fire was quenching:
   For doubt, and fear, and hope,
With fitful gleams the heart dividing,
However guileless and confiding,
   Must make the spirit droop.

From that fair season when the early
Bridegroom Sun lifts up the pearly
    Gauze that veils his bride
The Earth, to that when robed in splendours
His looks benignant back she renders,
    And smiles with matron pride—

From the bright day-star's first uprising,
When the gay lark, her pinions poising,
    Her morning hymn hath made,
Until, with softening radiance dipping,
His parting beams, the head-lands tipping,
    On distant Marfydd fade—

From spring to autumn—morn to even—
Had Gwendda's heart and mind be given
    To one pervading thought;
And from her toils each moment sparing,
Where last she saw him disappearing,
    The Hunter's form she sought.

It was a lofty rock projecting,
The narrow cottaged ledge protecting,
    And at its rugged base,
On a few scattered crags out-jutting,
The shepherd found a scanty footing,
    Or those who urged the chase.

There, as an April day was fleeting,
After such brief, impassioned meeting
  As stolen love supplies,
A last short pause, as met their burning
Lips, and at their rocky turning,
  He vanished from her eyes!

On the loved, dreaded spot she gazed,
  Her young hopes fading, day by day,
And as her tearful eyes she raised,
  Unerringly they turned that way.

But what can paint her wild surprise,
  Convulsive start, and piercing scream,
At what now met her straining eyes
  And scared her spirit like a dream?

There, on that very mountain shelf,
  Where last she saw him wave his hand
Ere yet he vanished—lo, himself!—
  In life and truth she saw him stand!

Seemed that he made a moment's pause,
  To contemplate, yet not to press,
Upon the touching scene whose cause,
  Oh, can we doubt, he half could guess.

How could he fail, whose soul had pined
　　The absence of its dearer part,
Which nothing did but closer bind
　　That ever loved one to his heart?

No, Gwendda, it is not thy doom,
　　For whatsoe'er misfortunes born,
To feel thy young affection's bloom
　　Nipp'd by the chilling blight of scorn.

One look its deep mysterious spell
　　Across the gulf of absence threw,
And worked the joyful word to tell,
　　From each to each, that both were true.

In neither did the other see
　　A change, but deeper lines of thought;
Such as by added years must be,
　　And graver scenes and musings, wrought.

O love, thou ray of light divine,
　　Down from God's cloud-encompassed throne
On MAN, the outcast, sent to shine,
　　And show him he is still HIS own—

Thy strength can break the hardest doom,
　　Thy weakness mould the sternest will;

Thy radiance gild the deepest gloom :
Thine essence doth all nature fill !

Within thy sacred presence quail
   All selfish passions, mean desires :
The smaller virtues even " pale,"
   Before thy face, their "lessened fires ! "

The careful mother this-ward swayed,
   The re-united left alone;
Resolved, by questions deeply weighed,
   The short remission to atone.

Without the cot, in thoughtful mood,
   (While on the pair retired within
Nor she nor we will yet intrude,)
   She pondered how she should begin.

But ere her plan assumed a shape
   To satisfy her prudent mind,
Down from the crags with hasty step,
   A shepherd youth her counsels joined.

'Twas Rhirid from the crowning feast
Returning, with the breathless haste
Of one who adds to travel's toil,
Some tangled tidings to uncoil :

So met they both with equal need,
To get their minds from burdens freed.

" Mother, I have Prince Madog seen,
And such a wondrous tale I ween—"

" Nay, nay, my son, I know it well.
Of gauds and glories wouldst thou tell ;
But this may wait—of kings and courts
For us to hear it less imports
Than nearer matters—Listen then—
Thou know'st the Hunter of the Glen—"

" Of him I speak ; this stranger brave—"

" Thou spak'st of Madog—Dost thou rave ?—
Hear what I say, it touches near
On all to us that should be dear :
Thy sister harboured in her breast
The memory of our hunter guest :
But he, I judged, had long forgot
His visits to our mountain cot,
Till now, when I was pressing mild
A mother's counsels on her child,
The noble stranger, as of yore—"

She stopped; for now the cottage door
Unclosed, and straightway, hand in hand,
The youthful pair before them stand.
The Hunter's face was grave and calm;
A flush of not unpleased alarm
Suffused the maiden's cheek:
The mother's wise intent to speak
Was stifled in a sudden shriek
From Rhirid—"Yes 'tis even so!"
And to the stranger bending low,
With reverend knee upon the sward,
He hailed him, "Madog, Sovereign Lord!"

" Rise, Rhirid, I receive thy troth;
And, mother, rise; I owe ye both
Good thanks; and something did I owe
This lovely maid—the cause to show
Of much that much it boots her know.
A prince's duty scarce admits
The softer scenes, except by fits;
And yet more rarely should they yield
To such, who sovereign empire wield.
The rites thou saw'st performed to-day
On me those sterner duties lay,
And here forbid my longer stay."

A PRINCE OF WALES

LONG AGO.

CANIAD THIRD.

CANIAD III.

WHAT deep analogies the thoughtful find
Between the world of matter and of mind.
A mountain is ambition, with its head
Above the clouds, but of the storm in dread:
The lowly vale 's humility—a river,
The course of time, still flowing ever—ever—
But merging in the deep and boundless sea,
The emblem fit of vast Eternity!
But where 's a type in nature's varied range,
For envy, hatred, malice, or revenge?
No outward symbol can of such be gleaned;
No dwelling have they but in man and fiend.
Their track, indeed, is all too plainly shown;
In blood, wars, tumults, treasons, mark it down:
While mixing up with some fair-seeming thing,
They take its hue, as deadly snakes that cling
Around some tropic tree, and look the same—
Right, justice, glory, valour, deathless fame—
Thus lurk they, undetected, till they breathe,
From venom'd jaws, the fumes that kill or scathe.

What was it else but jealous hate,
Disguised in policy of state,

That urged, fair Queen, thy bitter fate,
   And cast a foul disgrace
Upon an else-wise honoured name,
That neither wisdom, world-wide fame,
A people's gratitude that claim,
   Nor time can e'er efface?

And, oh, a direr instance still—
'T was envy worked for man the ill
That did the world with mischief fill,
   And worketh evermoe:
The being who had lost, through pride,
His first estate, could not abide
The sight of joy, to him denied,
   And changed that joy to woe.

Envy, with the scorpion sting,
Foul, envenomed, wretched thing,
Other passions have their fling
   On other objects round;
Rage seeking blood, and avarice pelf,
But thou upon thy victim self
   Inflict'st thy deepest wound!

Profits it touch, taste, ear, or eye,
Thy fell desires to gratify?—
Some faint excuse may such supply
   When passions wild enthral;

But thine unhallowed appetite
Not e'en the throbs of sense incite,
Nor joys of taste, touch, hearing, sight,
   Appease its carrion call.

O Envy, mischief is thy food,
Good is thine evil, and thine evil good.
Upon thine horrid altar all that's fairest
Must fall—the refuse and the vile thou sparest.
   Could no meaner sacrifice
   Thy dread demands suffice,
Than he, the bravest and the best—
Nor any for arch-priest,
At such a rite. but he—the nearest?

Ah well, my tale must speed along,
Through good and evil, right and wrong:
   Those who trill the storied song,
   Discordant notes must oft prolong.

View we now a stately hall—
   Chiefs are met in solemn feast;
Ranged upon the trophied wall,
   Their warlike weapons rest.
While 'neath the fretted roof impending,
Banners broad are o'er them bending,

Whose various devices show
What chieftain's armour gleams below.

Nor chiefs alone, who weapons wield
    Of carnal warfare, find their place;
But glitters many a shield,
Upon whose chequered field
    Emblems more holy share the space:
And which o'er-head high jewelled mitres grace.

And notably Cadwallawn, thine,
Cognate of the royal line,
And of such saintly virtue deemed,
That fitting most it seemed,
    Thou should'st preside in Enlli's isle,
Beneath whose sod so many saints[13] are laid,
That potent charms and amulets are made
    Of its thrice precious soil.

Through land's worst perils—ocean's rage,
The sanctuary's claims engage,
    From climes remote and near,
The live and dead from earliest ages
To make these arduous pilgrimages,

---

[13] 20,000 saints are said to have been buried in Bardsey Island.

Not 'r' Eifl's deserts, steep and drear—
No season of the changeful year—
Not all the terrors can dismay
Of Ceredigion's treach'rous bay,[14]
Whose waters, by a drunkard urged
To burst their bounds, seven towns submerged—
    Not distance, danger, nor delay
    May mar that project dear.
Oft on the steeps that hem around
Dark Nigel's port, and that dread sound
Through which the billows boil and bound,
For lingering weeks they wait the hour—
Crowds of the living at the shrine
To kneel; and many a funeral line;
    Till favouring gales may waft them o'er.
While, still more fearful, round the shore,
Toss'd in their barks, are crowds that pour
From Armorica's kindred coasts,
And Scotia's—Ireland's—Norway's hosts !—
Among them many an unsought grave
Is found beneath th' unpitying wave :
Together mourned and mourners sleep,
Among the "treasures of the deep."
Ah, empty honours—dearly bought—

---

[14] Seithenyn, in a drunken fit, had the dykes cut: 5th century.

Ah, blinded zeal, that profits nought!
View now the goal so keenly sought—
One crumbling fragment marks the spot:
For thronging worshippers, the eye
Has only solitude: for wailing dirge,
The listener but the sea-bird's cry,
For organ's peal, the ever booming surge!
What wonder the device should be,
On Enlli's shield, the heaving sea,
Above, an outstretched arm and hand,
And on the scroll—AT THY COMMAND!

  But volumes scarce could tell,
   And nothing could describe,
  But learned herald's skill,
   The arms of every tribe
  That did so nobly fill
   Each " coign of 'vantage ground "
That on those regal walls was found.

To head the honoured roll what name
Precedence may more duly claim,
 Than Hwfa's of Llys Llifon?—
 To whose proud hand 't was given,
 When Gwynedd crowned her king,
 The sacred badge to bring?

There stood thy storm-defying oak,[15]
Unheedful of the iron stroke,
   As when the Norman battle-axe
     The sapling ranks was felling,
   Thou stood'st unmoved its fierce attacks,
     O Carwed of Twrcelyn,
   What time in Eulo's forest met
   Great Owain and Plantagenet,
     And Cymru's valiant bands,
      Back from their mountain lands,
   The tide of conquest set!

There were Cregênan's[16] knotted snakes:
   The ermine-bearing crows of Bran;[17]
He from that chief his lineage takes
   Who first imperial Rome o'er-ran,
And gently pulled the venerable hairs
Of Conscript Fathers on their curule chairs
Scarce could the wonder-struck barbarian hold
Forms so august for men of mortal mould.[18]

---

[15] His arms were an oak crossed by two arrows.

[16] Owain ab Bradwen, head of one of the fifteen tribes—arms, gules —three snakes in a triangular knot, arg.

[17] Llywarch ab Brän, descended from Brennus—arms, three crows with ermine in their bills.

[18] It is related that when the British Chieftain, Brennus, at the head of the Gallic host, made his victorious entry into Rome the senators, having determined upon dying at their posts, assumed their senatorial

There was thy chevron. Maelog Grwm.[19]
Whose ground of deepest gloom
Three Cherubim illume.
Like those who, as the Patriarch dreamed[20]
In the dark desert, seemed
Upon the mystic ladder's side,
In bright succession, up and down to glide.

How leaped the heart—how flashed the eye
Of Gwynedd's champions, to descry
The blazoned signs that must recall
Such glorious memories to all!

But there was one—ah, me! what bard
Without a sigh—a blush—a tear,
Might tell the cause—or who might hear
Why thy escutcheon was reversed—

costume, and, seated in their curule chairs, thus awaited their fate. When Breunus and his barbarian followers discovered them thus arranged with all the dignified composure suitable to their office, unmoved by the terrors by which they were surrounded, they regarded them as something more than human—in fact, they considered them to be gods. From the mode which Breunus adopted, however, for ascertaining how far they possessed the susceptibilities of mortals, our countryman appears to have been quite free from any superstitious fears on this occasion, for, having recovered from the astonishment which their appearance first inspired, he proceeded to pull their beards for that purpose. Breunus lived in the fourth century before the Christian Era

[19] Head of one of the fifteen tribes—arms, arg. on a chev. sab. three angels.

[20] See Genesis, chap. xxviii.

Thy banner trampled. and—accursed
 Thy name and tribe, O Nefydd Hardd?[21]
  Long shall Nantconwy mourn
  Her flag of honour torn,
And levelled with the dust!
  Yet less could not atone
  A crime that stands alone
Upon the dark record, and ever must—
No, not the expiatory towers of fair Llanrwst!

  What though, with liberal care,
  Kind nature did prepare
  A casket more than fair,
   Thy blackened soul to hide—
  Had she more lavish been,
  And given thee a mien,
  Such as has not been seen,
   Since victor squadrons wide,
  Drew back to make a road
  For one who seemed a god—
  Sandde,[22] of matchless shape,
  The slaughter to escape

[21] Nefydd Hardd, or, the Handsome, head of one of the fifteen tribes, to whom Owain Gwynedd entrusted his son Idwal, and who had him murdered. by his son Dunawd, at Cwm Idwal. Another son of Nefydd's in expiation of the crime, founded the Church of Llanrwst.

[22] Sandde, one of the twenty-four sons of Llywarch Hên—so beautiful that, at the battle of Camlan, the enemy's ranks made way for him to pass through, thinking he was a god. Only two more escaped that battle.

>   Of Camlan's bloody day—
>   E'en such celestial grace
>   Could ne'er the stain efface
>   On thy foul name that lay!

And there was yet another dire mishap—
Among these high achievments was a gap;—
That morn had seen th' heraldic blaze complete;
Each chieftain's armour marked his destined seat.
High o'er the centre of the dais,
Two royal 'scutcheons had their place:
The monarchs of two neighbouring states, allied
In friendship, should in arms be side by side.

>   Now when the banquet smoked—
>   When guests had been invoked—
>   When forth the heralds came,
>   Their lineage to proclaim—
>   And bards in lofty choirs.
>   Had tuned their triple wires,
>   To celebrate their feats—
>   As to their chosen seats
>   The marshals of the feast
>   Conduct each honoured guest—
>   When to the high alcove
>   All eyes instinctive turn.

For two insignia raised above,
   But one they now discern.
The Powis royal trophy 's gone,
And Owain Gwynedd's stands alone!
Ah, doubly so, for soon 't is known,
The monarch, bent with age and toil.
And staggered by that morning's moil,
Had failed e'er night, and anxious fear
In all around, for life so dear,
Consigned him to the leech's care.

And, ah, yet worse—if worse could be—
Mischance that feast was doomed to see.—
   Its primal cause, adornment, soul,
   Was absent when the heraldic roll,
   With trumpet's blast and loud acclaim,
   Was answered with each knightly name.
   All silent was the mournful air—
   Madog of Maelor was not there!

Stripped of its glories, there was need
The festal rite should yet proceed;
Its presidency passed at once
Among the other royal sons.
And there was one the chance who viewed
As welcomed more to be than rued.

Not Iorwerth—he of speech was plain,
Renowned for valour more than brain,
With heart sincere, but rugged phrase,
He spoke his absent brother's praise.
It was not Hywel—he was gay
As birds who trill the joyous lay,
Through summer bowers the live-long day,
And he had been in foreign courts,
And he had basked 'neath softer skies;
Had couched the lance in royal sports,
And tuned the string where gentle eyes
Looked on, and gentle hands bestowed the prize;
Had learned among the Troubadours,
That praise and love and joy belong
Far less to thrones and kingly powers,
Than feats of arms and feats of song.
With full effusion, bardic skill,
He spoke, and brother's right good will:
And said, that, even in the face
    Of that tribunal high,
Where of the learn'd and tuneful race,
(Though one, alas, was not in place,)
    So many met his eye,
He should his daring hand have brought,
    To aid his heart and tongue,
In praising one whose praises ought

For ever to be sung ;
But he had made a solemn vow,[23]
To wake no lyric strain,
That had not Love for its refrain,
Until his duteous knee should bow
To the fair Princess, Yvar of Bretagne.

Thus spake chivalric Hywel, warrior-bard—
From every corner of the hall were heard
Responsive acclamations all around :
Soft sparkling mead the mighty hirlas crowned ;
Applausive symphonies swept through
The spacious vault, whose thousand coigns
Of fretted ornament renew
The notes, and every whisper joins.
   All narrow emulations cease—
     Vouchsafe the graduated bards—
   Cedivor.[24] Meilor. Ieuan. Rhys—
     To honorary skill their high awards

'T was Uthyr's turn—his tone and speech
   Were quiet, strait and unrehearsed ;

---

[23] Such vows were usual in the age of romance and chivalry; they were thought very complimentary to the ladies in whose favour they were made

[24] C, called ek in the British language, is always hard, like Saxon k.

Yet there was somewhat seemed to reach
  More deeply than appeared at first.
Confirming all that they had heard
  From those who 'd touched the theme before,
Of Madog's praise—to every word
  He amplest testimony bore.
About his high deserts in war
  And things of war, it scarce became
A humble follower, placed so far
  Behind as he was, to declaim.
But in that proud assemblage sate
  Of hoary veterans not a few,
The impress of whose words of weight
  Would stamp his weaker words as true.
Of all the qualities that go
  To form a leader, was there one
That some there present could not show
  Bright in the youthful hero shone?
Enquired they if in pressing urgence,
  Sacrificing scruples small,
He prompt could weigh the great emergence?—
  Answer Ithel, Lord of Iâl!
Minded he Glyndwrddu's smiling[25]
  Harvests given to the flame,

[25] Glyndwrddu was the heritage and seat of the Lords of Iâl: now Yale.

When of the Norman hordes defiling
  Through Berwyn's passes tidings came?
Did they of discipline enquire?—
  They all with Iorwerth would agree,
That discipline exalted higher,
  Or carried further, could not be.
He would bethink him of the day
  When, levelled Aberystwith's tower.
At mercy lay—a tempting prey—
  Padarn's rich shrine, and Ystrad Flür.[26]
But, lo, or e'er his hardy bands
  With these could compensate their toils,
Down came the Chief-supreme's commands,
  Who says, " Forbear the sacred spoils ! "
The voice was as a demi-god's—
  Like to the voice they heard that day;
When such a being looks or nods,
  All lower beings must obey.
Like Deity enshrouded now,
  The hero leaves his empty shrine,
To which his worshippers may bow—
  Himself unseeing and unseen.

He spake—the words were words of praise;
But yet the thoughts they seemed to raise,

[26] Two monasteries, near Aberystwith.

As glances through the lofty hall,
Were lifted toward the vacant stall,
O'er which, midst armour, meetly grouped,
The Griffin banner drooped—
Those thoughts in some seemed not unmixed
With somewhat that their course perplexed.
And all those glances did not shine
With influences the most benign.
A shade came over Iorwerth's brow,
And under it the deep'ning glow
Told of a passing inward throe.
And though on Ithel's swarthy cheek
   Already time had 'gan to strew
   His snows on curls of raven hue,
   The tell-tale tide shone blazing through,
Nor seemed alone about to speak—
   Low sounds, like those that on the air
   Its viewless undulations bear.
Of distant tempest telling,
   Unshaped to words, the chieftain breathed—
   With warlike instinct inly writhed
   His sons, and half their swords unsheathed—
Young Hwfa and Llewellyn—

   As when at summer noon,
Upon the glassy surface of the lake,

Some plashing drops its stilly smoothness break,
Which from their skirts dark threatening vapours shake,
  But they pass over soon—
So was the banquet's easy flow
Disturbed by eddies from below:
But well did he who stirred them know
How far their troubling force might go;
He knew the times were only full
To set the wires, but not to pull.
He caused, with seeming unconcern,
The spirit of the hour to turn;
And summoned other spirits up—
The spirit of the harp and the spirit of the cup.
He turned a look to the gallery high,
  In which the bardic college sate,
And it was caught by the searching eye
  Of one who looks could well translate.
The signal reached the gallery's shade,
And Cedivor came forth to the balustrade:
  His dark locks rolled beneath
  The gilded oaken wreath
That marked the highest bardic grade;
  His look was calm and deep,
  Like the mountain torrent's sleep
  Before its maddened leap.

Then on his statued frame
    'Gan inspiration pour,
And then the boiling rapids came,
    And then the thundering roar!

He sung Gods—Fathers—Heroes—Kings—
The gorgeous strain that ever brings
The mead of praise to him who sings.
    The noble theme he sung
    Of Britain's rise and root ;
    And that resounding tongue
    That never shall be mute—[27]
    He sung the dawn of Britain's day—
        The semi-mythic ages tracked,
    Before the tri-partitioned sway
        Of Lloegrin—Camber—Albanact—[28]
He touched, with all an artist's skill,
The dim, but giant forms, that fill
The bright horizon of the past,
When morning's lengthened beams are cast.

Men of wisdom—men of power—
Huw Gadarn—Prydain—Beli Mawr,[29]

---

[27] There is an ancient prophecy that the British language shall last for ever.

[28] These three Chiefs were the first who divided England, Scotland, and Wales : whence the names Lloegyr, Cambria, and Albany.

[29] Three prominent characters in early British history.

Such names as pagan gratitude would swell
Into the ranks of classic heaven or hell.
The poet's fancy kindled as he neared
Epochs less distant and yet more revered,
If warmed at heathen wisdom—virtue—rites—
Much more at Christian sages—martyrs—knights;
A Cattwg's[30] learning, and a Beuno's[31] zeal—
A chaste Gwenfrewi's[32] holy powers to heal,
From that pure fount, the emblem of her soul.
Whose virtues make her faithful votaries whole.

How glowed the lay, how thrilled the wire,
When ARTHUR's glories waked the lyre!

Beamed every eye—hushed every sound—
   Listened with bated breath the throng—
Paused the deep hirlas in its round,
   When Arthur was the theme of song.

The flower of knighthood, when that name
   The symbol was of manly worth,
Of valour, wisdom, spotless fame—
   Beloved of Heaven—revered on earth.

---

[30] A celebrated sage, the founder of a college in South Wales.
[31] St. Beuno, a holy man of the 6th century, the founder of a college at Clynnog, the fine Church of which remains.
[32] *Winifred* in the Saxon tongue; her legend and fountain at Holywell are known.

A king, when in that title met
  The essences of all that fill
The ideal of Heaven's delegate—
  The force of laws, the people's will.

For, know all we of modern days,
  Who boast of liberty and laws,
Our British Fathers share the praise—
  They edged the sword that freedom draws.

And though it rusted long beneath
  Unblest dominion, feudal strife;
It burst, in time, the crumbling sheath,
  And, flaming, guards that tree of life.

This is a goodly plant, " whose seed
  Is in itself upon the earth; "
United streams through ages feed
  Its growth from its primeval birth.

How futile, then, the hopes and toil
  That, frantic, wrench some full grown tree,
Transplant it to repugnant soil,
  And name it after LIBERTY!

For though awhile its head it rears,
  Its sapless boughs are bare of fruit:

And soon the eddying tempest tears,
    Or drought dries up its shallow root.

Deep in the storm-made mountain cleft,
    True freedom strikes its firmest hold;
There, clinging, were its votaries left
    When Saxon tides o'er Britain rolled.

And now was struck a trembling string—
    A chord of mingled good and ill—
A nation's fall—a dastard king[33]—
    A remnant true to freedom still.

Round nature's citadel of snows
    They saved a strip of sterile earth,
Undesecrate by heathen foes,
    To guard the altar and the hearth.

And now the echo of the song
Was " Cymro[34] true ! " and " Cymru strong ! "
Now, severed from the southern race,
It was the bardic task to trace
A nation's deeds, whose narrow space

---

[33] Gwrtheyrn, in Saxon, *Vortigern*.
[34] *Cymro* is "the inhabitant of *Cymru*," which is the name of the country; thence *Cymraeg*, "of the country" In like manner as, *Briton, Britain, British*.

Was not the measure of its soul :
For on its kingly roll
Were names that would deserve a place
In triumphs or of peace or war—
A Rhodri Mawr, a Hywel Ddà.
The first by martial genius tamed
    Of adverse tribes the senseless rage ;
The last, conflicting customs framed
    Into a code of practice sage :

All this close following on the age
    When Alfred laboured to assuage
His country's wrongs—her ways reclaimed,
And based that social fabric now so famed,
Whose fair proportions fitly rise—
    Foundations wide extend, and deep :
    Thence grades ascend, nor rough nor steep ;
Its apex 'spiring to the skies,
Round which the tempests harmless sweep,
That lay less solid structures in a heap.

Long may it stand, as now it stands,
In its strong quietness—the glory of all lands !
Thrice blest the bard who such a theme commands.
    That theme Cedivor lacked,
    But with a lyrist's tact,
    He flies from act to act,

Of heroes, poets, kings;
And from the illumined haze
Of fable, to the blaze
Of glorious recent days,
　　The tuneful record brings:
Till to the climax' height,
He bears his bardic flight,
And sound and silence both unite
To mark his hearers' deep delight,
　　When "Owain's praise" he sings!

'T were bootless to compare[85]
Aught for which moderns care—
Applause of senates, or the meed of song—
　　With the effect intense
　　On mind and soul and sense,
Of Bardic skill our primal sires among.
　　　Not all the love, the ire,
　　　The softness or the fire,
　　　Waked by Timotheus' lyre
In classic times, were prompter or more strong:

---

[85] The powerful effects of the songs of the Bards among the early Celtic nations is well known. Peace, war, treaties, and every other social and political crisis, were affected by these popular agencies. Even as late as the times of Glyndwr this still prevailed, and the Bard of that chieftain exercised a potent influence, which Mrs. Hemans has availed herself of in her beautiful words to the air of "The rising of the Lark."

And well Cedivor knew
The time for striking true,
When Madog's absence threw
A cast that had not happed, nor might, for long.

As poet and historian now,
He neared the touchstone meet to show
　　The mettle of his art—
The glories of the current reign
Ignobly told, those might complain
　　Who in them bore a part.

But if a bard[86] of other days,
And tongue and nation, felt the " praise
　　Of Owain swift and strong "
Inspire his soul, how much the more,
On such coeval poets pour
　　The fairest streams of song!

He traced his high and pure descent,
Which lacked no link, and knew no taint;
　　For aye, on either parent's side ;
From sovereign stocks the grafts were lent,

---

[86] Gray, in his fragmentary ode, beginning—
　　" Owen's praise demands my song;
　　　Owen swift, and Owen strong!"

From Powis, Arfon, Dyfed, Gwent,[87]
Or over seas; for well 't was known,
In Cymru none could mount a throne
    Who wedded not a royal bride.

'T was not enough for British king
A spotless pedigree to bring,
He must provide for handing down
A lineage faultless as his own.

And here with art that looked like chance,
He took occasion to enhance
The aged king's paternal care.
That who succeeded him might share
His kingdom with a royal fair,
For else he could not be his heir.
How much it touched them then to heal
The Powis breach, which all must feel,
Not only risked their monarch's life,
But, after that, internal strife.
Avert it, Heaven!—such double dole—
Might Owain reach the utmost goal

---

[87] These were often, during the changes of dynasties in Cymru, distinct sovereign houses: at other times they merged one into the others, in such unsettled times. It is this capricious and changeable circumstance in the rules of succession that is considered to have been a chief element of the weakness and downfall of Welsh independence.

Of human days; and when his sun
Its glorious course at length had run,
Rise up another star, whose ray
Might guide them through as bright a day!

Here was a stanza in the lay,
   At which the soaring strain was checked.
To give the bard a moment's stay,
   And the effusion more effect.

And when, in bold prophetic flight,
   He called the morning star to rise,
With salutation seemed to light
   On Uthyr's form his diamond eyes,
Where, as by fascination, turned the rest likewise.

A moment spell-bound seemed the host—
   The harp's vibrations faintly rung—
When filled the air a trumpet's blast,
   And wide the ponderous portal swung;
Then, like the morning rising in the sky,
Young Madog mounted to his tribune high.

Seemed like a vision more than truth,
The presence of the godlike youth—
The silent wonder through the hall
More like a brief enchantment's thrall·
But soon his voice the real did recall.

With princely courtesy he spoke,
Did freely their excuse invoke,
For failure in the festal tryst,
By which less they than he had missed.
About the cause he nothing said,
That thus his coming had delayed:
But to his young cup-bearer signed,
   That he the Chiefs would pledge;
Then on the cup his head inclined
   And kissed its silver edge.

'T was now for them to pledge in turn,
And haply Madog might discern
Some looks among them strange and stern,
Whose meaning he some day might learn.

But now he gave the lesser thought
To such fore-tokens, for that fraught
His spirit was with other doubt;
And salutation duly paid,
   With answer due from every chief,
The sad announcement then he made.
   That bowed his soul with filial grief.

The sudden faintness that withheld
   The king from sitting at the feast.

The leech's skill had not dispelled,
    But coming night had still increased.

Befitting, then, it was to stay
    At once all further festive rite,
Until at some more happy day,
    The king restored should such invite.

A PRINCE OF WALES

LONG AGO.

—

CANIAD FOURTH.

.

CANIAD IV.

WIDELY may meditation range
Upon the mystery of CHANGE—
A common sound of daily use,
But full of harmonies abstruse,
And capable to exercise
Our thoughts and fancies, ears and eyes.

Behold the winter tree—nor hue
Nor form commends it to our view:
The winds, as through its shreds they scream,
Lashed into harsher fury seem:
View it again, when mantling o'er,
Bright blossoms burst from every pore—
Looks it not " something new and strange?"
It is the mystery of *Change!*

Seems the poor infant on the knee
   Its feeble breath about to yield—
Do we the statesman—warrior—see—
   To shake the senate or the field?

Nor in the outer world alone
   This silent wonder works its way—
Thought, habits, manners, change their tone
   From year to year, from day to day.

Had we permission to restore
  E'en a departed saint to life,
'T is question if the gift would more
  A blessing be, or source of strife.

Could Alfred walk the earth again—
  Would he congenial objects find?
Or would the stones on Sarum's plain
  Alone speak homeward to his mind?
    Ah, little else would be as he had left behind!

Except the solid mass that bears
  These fleeting things upon its breast,
There 's nothing but that largely shares
  This general sentence of *Unrest*.

'T is to the features, soft or stern,
  Impressed on our Great Mother's face,
That we alone can safely turn
  The REAL of our world to trace.

But for such land-marks on the shore
  Of the dim PAST's receding sea,
Wide we should drift the winds before,
  Doubtful of all *identity*.

So stand the cliffs—so booms the surf,
   As when invading Cæsar came—
Smooth angles on a hillock's turf [37]
   Some furlongs inland bear his name.
   Is there aught else remains the same?

And can the mind such spots survey,
   Nor fill the living picture in
With every form and tint that may
   Recal the scenes that once have been?

Arrange we thus the tract that leads
Towards Mona's shores from Maelor's meads—
Join we the escorts that convey
A royal pilgrim on his way—
They bear the king, returning now,
In part restored, to Aberffraw.[38]
With frequent rests, by easy moves,
He thinks to reach the place he loves,
Ere yet descends the final blow
That lays both Prince and peasant low.
Dejected at the turn malign
Of late events, at Seiriol's shrine,[40]

---

[38] Cæsar's camp, near Folkstone.

[39] Owain Gwynedd's palace in Anglesea, where he lived. He lies buried in the Cathedral of Bangor.

[40] At Priestholme, now Puffin Island, near Anglesey, one of the most venerated retreats of the saints of the Britons.

And every intermediate place
Where saintly foot had left its trace,
He vowed a visit in his path,
To deprecate the heavenly wrath.

One princely son his march attends,
The rest dispersed on various ends.

Madog his fortress court maintains,
(Which still his honoured name retains),
To guard, as erst, the frontier plains.
Homeward his way took Iorwerth bold
To Dolwyddelan's Castle hold:[39]
His duty was to keep in awe
Wild mountain tribes who scoff at law.
At Uther's suit had been decreed
That he to Powis should proceed,
And fitting mediations try
To reconcile their old ally.
Though scorned, no whit did he despair
Of winning yet the royal fair:
For his the gift of looking through
The human mind: and well he knew

---

[41] The remains of this stronghold still exist Here also was born his son, Llywellyn the Great.

That, often, disappointed love
With suicidal vengeance strove
To mitigate the keenest smart
Can rankle in the female heart.
Thus royally espoused, when soon
In nature's course was void the throne,
He deemed the purpose all complete,
Long planned his brother to defeat.

Iorwerth 't was known had lost his right,
For Nature, with a step-dame's spite,
Had marred his face,[42] nor would permit
That he on Gwynedd's throne should sit,
However valiant else, and fit.
From times remote, the law's decree—
A royal spouse; a form from blemish free.
And for the rest, young Hywel's bent
To aught than to intriguing leant:
The cares of state, or any care,
Too irksome were for him to share.
Now by the royal litter's side,
The escort's chief, 't is his to ride.
And oft he lightly caracoles,
Or gay refrain or ballad trolls,

[42] He was called Drwyndwm, from the defect in his nose. *See* Williams's "Enwogion Cymru."

The journey's tedium to beguile,
And weakness' fret, and age's toil.

And when the grave procession came
  To holy shrine, or cross, or spring,
Would draw a bow at sylvan game,
  Or tune the crwth's[43] melodious string.

And while within, on lowly knee,
  The king and his attendants bent,
Some tale or catch of jonglerie
  All joyous on the gale was sent.

Thrilled the soft cadence on the breeze
That stirred the feathery birchen trees,
Crisping the surface of the wave
That back their drooping image gave;
And floating upwards to the edge
Of vast Eglwyseg's[44] strated ridge.
Whose buttressed fronts appear to stand
As much by Art's as Nature's hand;
The base of some hugh tower whose top
Beneath the skies might scarcely stop;

---

[43] A small harp.
[44] These are limestone formations, with traces of water-line, sea-shells, and other indications of having been the bed of an ocean.

Like that on which, in Shinar's plain,[45]
Presumptuous builders toiled in vain.
There stood they, solemn, stark, and grey,
As now they stand, upon the day
When Hywel trilled his lightsome lay.
Ere Dee's dark eddies in their curve,
Had learned industrial ends to serve :
Or his more wide impetuous flow
Was banked those wondrous curbs[46] below,
That stretch through air their mighty span,
At bidding of "the pigmy, man !"
Ere yet his voices, soft or strong,
Had mingled with the engine's clang,
Or his bright foam-wreaths, as they broke,
Been tarnished by surphureous smoke.

And e'en before the sacred fane[47]
Whose fragments have for ages lain,
In verdant hillocks, mouldering cast
A touching memory of the past—
Ere this first rose, in modest pride,
Like the veiled splendours of a bride,

---

[45] See Genesis chap. xi.
[46] Pont-y-Cysyllte, and the Viaduct lower down, which span the valley of the Dee.
[47] Valle Crucis Abbey, founded A. D. 1200, by Madog ab Grüffydd, grandson of Owain Gwynedd.

All virgin white above the screen,
By nature draped, her mantle green—
Ere yet the bones[48] that lately lay
Revealed a while, in face of day,
Had worn the garb of life, and stood
And moved—a thing of flesh and blood—
And pondered deep in thought to build
That Abbey in the sylvan wild,
Where requiems for a sinful soul
Might through its echoing arches roll
" For ever "—so the statutes ran—
FOR EVER—what a word for *man!*

Before all this—but not before
A lofty croslet,[49] sculptured o'er,
Had stretched its slender arms above
The summits of a sacred grove,
During a lapse of time as long
As now has passed since Hywel sung.

To thought—to pen—how short appears
The step across twelve hundred years—

---

[48] This skeleton, lying before the high altar, was found in the excavations lately completed for clearing the area of the Abbey Church: it was re-interred immediately.

[49] This is Eliseg's pillar, commemorating the death of that Chief in a battle fought in this spot, and erected by Cyngen, his great-grandson. —7th century.

But if that cross could tell the tale
Of all that even in that vale
In nature's change hath had its part,
Or that small world the human heart,
The gayest sure would sigh—the firmest start!

It speaks—that emblem of our faith—
Of duty, valour, sorrow, death—
And could the relics that beneath
This valley's surface heave the sod,
Spring forth, obedient to a nod,
Like those that scattered, frail and dry[50]
Rose up before the Prophet's eye,
In all their warlike panoply—
Could blast of trumpet—clash of shield,
Resound across that silent field—
And flashing spear and gleaming crest
Light the deep shadows of Llangwest—
What glowing interest would that scene invest!

'T is to divert awhile the thought
Of struggling MAN, with burdens fraught,
Of gain—ambition—worldly ends—
The spread of acres or of friends—

[50] Ezekiel chap. xxxvii

Or close appliance to detail
Of progress on a wider scale,
Which in the name of public weal
Absorbs too much the spirit's zeal—
To turn his energies intense,
At times, away from things of sense,
That in some hearts the ruling Mind,
Which hath to every part assigned
Its proper working in His plan,
From herb to cedar—mite to Man,
Implants a longing to controul
And upward turn the human soul,
Ask not why such their musings give
To public view—ask why they live—
Imbibe their food, or draw their breath—
'T is *instinct*—to suppress it—*death*—
'T is not that they would arrogate
A greater share of worth or weight
Than those to whom they thus impart
The fulness of a loving heart!
In ages distant, dark and rude,
These influences were understood:
'T was felt that some restraining force
Was well to check man's headlong course,
To soften—mitigate—refine—
And keep his image still *divine*.

And minds have been forthcoming still,
This gentle mission to fulfil.
For this did reverend elders pour
In *triads* forth their treasured lore—
For this have bards, in every age,
Joined fables gay to maxims sage :
To lift the soul. the fancy warm,
Make duty please, and wisdom charm.
When poets feigned that Orpheus' lute
Soothed into softness man and brute—
Made cities rise, and golden grain,
Where savage stillness wont to reign,
Their types were scarce too bold or free
To paint the Muse's ministry.
The working of her inward fires,
Called AWEN by our British sires,
In youthful Hywel found their vent.
As o'er his slender crwth he bent,
Against a rocky jut reclined,
Where scarce a kid might footing find.

The progress of the holy vow
Had brought the royal pilgrims now
Beyond the regions where the Dee
Drives his dark billows wide and free ;

And left behind the sacred plain
Whose sight waked thoughts of joy and pain :
And that bright morn that lately rose
So gay, but darkened ere the close.

Far in the trackless waste that spreads
Up from Edernion's laughing meads,
Where moor on moor in ridges heaves
Like the dark swell of ocean waves,
A spot there was from days of eld,
In something more than reverence held—
An awe, a dread—'t was scarce known what,
Or why—was fastened to the spot ;
For superstition less requires
Than faith to keep alive her fires:
'T was said the Druid's awful rite
Had sanctified, or stained the site ;
That human voices wont to groan,
And blood to tinge the altar stone,
At certain phases of the moon.
But doubtful howsoe'er its claim
To holiness. a holy name
Had to the mystic precinct clove—
'T was Llwyn Saint—The Holy Grove.[51]

[51] On the lefthand side of the Holyhead Road a mile beyond Glyn Bridge.

And here came peasant—chieftain—king—
Their prayers to make, their offerings bring.
And while, beneath the gloomy shade
Of oaks primeval, Owain made
Oblations rich, and while he prayed,
Young Hywel sought the desert wild,
Where rocks on rocks were hugely piled,
One of those bars whose stubborn force
Confronts a river in its course;
Which, as indignant at the check,
A deep remonstrance seems to make.
But all too wise to struggle long
With fate, majestic sweeps along,
And turning seems the calm to find
That waits the firm, well-balanced mind.

The spot inspired—the royal youth
Waked the soft warblings of the crwth—

HYWEL'S SONG.

"The Baron to the wars is gone.
  Ah, well-a-day—ah, well-a-day!
  His lady fair is left alone—
They had been wed but half a day.

The king was at the castle gate,
And with him all his armed array—
　For shame the baron could not wait,
Ah, well-a-day—ah, well-a-day!

Who shall to me your tidings bring?
Then frantic 'gan that Lady say;
　The Baron took the golden ring
From off her hand, ah, well-a-day!

Oh, cast that ring in the marble spring
On each return of our bridal day,
　And if I am slain it the image shall bring
Of him who hath slain me; ah, well-a-day!

A weary year hath passed away
And she casts in the crystal fount the ring,
　And in the wave, ah, well-a-day,
She sees the image of the King.

Then shrieked that lady with dismay,
And from the phantom turned to flee;
　But when she turned—ah, well-a-day,
The king was there upon his knee!

Your pardon, lady fair, I pray,
For love of you the deed I 've done,

And you shall sit—'t is well the day,
And reign with me upon the throne.

But from his grasp that lady bright
Plunged in the wave, ah, well-a-day,
  Her bridal robe of virgin white
Was purer than the crystal spray.

And as that morn comes round each year,
Clasped hand in hand, ah, well-a-day
  In bridal garb two forms appear
Bright smiling through the crystal spray."

The fading of an Autumn day
The pathos of the ballad-lay,
As died its cadences away,
In that impressive solitude,
Favoured the deep poetic mood;
And while the minstrel's finger still
Prolonged the harp's symphonious thrill,
His half-enwrapped, half-listening ear
A whispering answer seemed to hear.
It might but be his lyric strain
Rebounding from the rocks again—
Or the soft hushing of the wave
That shore-ward o'er the pebbles drave:

With breath suspended—ear intent,
Down from the dizzy crag he leant—
When, disentangled from the sound
Of song, or wind, or wave's rebound,
Upon the evening stillness passed
A wild and sweet but tuneless blast.
Now, like a lover's whispered vow,
It trembled on the air; and now,
In rolling volumes, soared on high
Like choirs of angels in the sky.
Then on the river's bosom sunk to die.

Young Hywel startled—charmed—amazed—
Above—around—beneath him gazed:
Then resolute at least to know
Whence those mysterious sounds could flow.
If they, indeed, were sounds of earth,
And owed not their aërial birth
To fairy—fancy—or a dream,
Or ghost, that restless o'er the stream,
Lamented the unhallowed grave
Its relics found beneath the wave,
With footstep light as mountain stag,
Swift bounded down from crag to crag;
E'en these, at times, his footing failed,

And on his headlong course he held
By clinging to the tendrils frail,
That over rocky 'scarpments trail,
Of fern, or eglantine, or heath,
And veil the yawning gulf beneath.
At times it shot athwart his brain
That all was but a snaring train,
Laid by the dæmons of the night,
In deeds of death that take delight.

All ye who know the rocky deep,
Where Geirw, startled from the sleep
Whose dreamy murmurs through the meads
His gentle course descending leads
From Ystrad, where, in youthful pride,
He wins the Bedrad for his bride,
Now dashes, with tumultuous din,
Down the abysses of the Glyn,[52]
Think not the scene ye there surveyed,
From prospect-seat, or esplanade,
Presents a picture such as when
Young Hywel wandered through the glen.

---

[52] Glyn Diffwys, a dell of great beauty and well known to the public from being traversed by the Holyhead road which runs in a nich cut out of the rock.

No chiselled bore, with sulph'rous train,
Had rent its mural mass in twain :
No travelled roadway smooth and wide,
Then gashed, 'mid height, its iron side :
Its gloomy gorge no dext'rous hand
With vaulted masonry had spanned—
Stern in primeval strength it stood,
As when emerging from the flood ;
Save that kind Nature's hand had strewed
Her graces o'er its features rude,
And clothed the slopes that shelved between
The bluffs and crags, with living green.

Propped, for an instant, on a ledge
That over-hung the chasm's edge,
And clinging to an ivy wreath,
Adventurous Hywel paused for breath.
And pondered, for a moment's space,
His downward progress to retrace ;
But now again, in breathings soft,
The mystic music streamed aloft.

"Now, by St. Cadfan," cried the youth,
"I 'll know the falsehood or the truth
Of this mysterious serenade :—
It may be, an imprisoned maid

Implores me, in these plaintive strains,
To free her from a tyrant's chains :
Nor take it, beauteous Yvar, ill,
That knightly devoir I fulfil ;
No treason is it to thy charms
That such a task my valour warms ! "

Nor doubt nor danger more he knew—
At thought of woman's wrongs he flew—
By swinging leap and flying tread
Attained at length the river's bed,
And landed where the narrow shore
Expanded wide and caverned o'er,
By working of the wintry flood,
Some steps above its level stood,
And offered access in and out,
When shrunk its bounds by summer drought ;
A grotto such as water sprite,
Or sleeping naiad might invite.

And here 't was plain that he would learn
What made his youthful fancy burn ;
For, as he neared the dim recess,
The music pealed with deeper stress ;
And lo, within, a stranger sight
Than prisoned maid, or water sprite—

Against the rugged rock-wall leant
A lonely harp, and o'er it bent,
All motionless, and pale, and wan,
With drooping head, an aged man :
No hand he lifted—touched no chord ;
Yet through the cave deep music poured.

Thrilled Hywel's fibres—reeled his brain—
He moved—drew back—approached again—
It was—it must be—Meurig Hên !

The gathering night-wind swept the cave
And made the old man's tresses wave—
But naught stirred else—with noiseless tread
The youth drew nigh—the bard was *dead!*

It was the fitful wind alone,
Had touched the harp, and waked its tone :
The stiffened hand all lifeless hung—
Glazed was the eye, and mute the tongue,
On which admiring crowds had hung !

With reverent step the prince withdrew—
Now twilight deepening shadows threw
Athwart the labyrinthine dell,
And it behoved young Hywel well

To clear its mazes e'er the night
In double doubt involved his flight—
The monarch, too, his duties done,
Would now await his absent son—
And much it touched his bardic pride
Such funeral honours to provide,
As might express his own and Cymru's grief
For him of seers the soul—of bards the chief!

    'T is now the twilight hour,
    In which the nameless Power
At the hill-altar, must be sought:—
    To the three-sided stone,
    Each votary alone
Must come, who of the future would be taught.
    But of these arches three
    One only must he see,
To enter two with dire mischance were fraught.

    Advanced, then, from his suite,
    Within the dim retreat,
    No sandals on his feet,
Ash-strewn his head that wont to wear a crown,
    Behold the aged Chief,
    Majestic in his grief,
Upon the cold, hard ground fall prostrate down!

And thus he made his prayer—
" O Thou dread Power, whate'er
The name that Thou would'st bear,
Or how, or when, or where
   Would'st worshipped be—
Shrouded in deepest gloom—
Deign to reverse the doom
That threatens to entomb
Our hopes. A king—a father bends the knee.
   Madog—the good—the wise—
   What madness blinds his eyes,
   That he should thus despise
And set at nought th' immutable decree ?—
   Refuse the lovely bride,
   Of kingly race allied,
   And risk that set aside
His else assured inheritance should be ?—
   His country then expose
   To fresh domestic woes,
   Designs of foreign foes,
And ills from which it scarcely yet is free.
Shall Madog to such chance the land deliver ? "

A low, soft voice pronounced, distinctly, "NEVER."

A PRINCE OF WALES

LONG AGO.

CANIAD FIFTH.

CANIAD V.

The Mountains of my Native Land
   Are fair and famous, every one;
Distinct doth each from other stand,
   With features specially its own.

Snowdon's claims are undisputed—
   Over all he reigns supreme:
Deep in every feeling rooted,
   Painter's vision—poet's dream!

Round him, grouped in all gradations,
   His coeval brothers rise,
Over boundless undulations
   Crags and peaks that pierce the skies.

Royal Dafydd and Llywellin,[53]
   From their carnedd, wide and far,
To the world for ever telling,
   Kings, like slaves, but mortal are,

---

[53] Carnedd Llywellin is the next highest mountain in Wales': near it is Carnedd Dafydd—they mark either the actual or supposed graves of those princes.

Far away o'er Meirion towers
    Star-led Idris' fabled seat.
Whence madness, death, or god-like powers
    Upon the dauntless watcher wait.[54]

Arren[55] dips his forky summit
    In the smooth translucent wave,
Where, beyond the reach of plummet,
    Arthur sleeps in crystal cave,

Till the destined hour for breaking
    Through the potent spell arrives,
And, from lengthened trance awaking,
    With his knights the warrior lives.

Parent proud of many waters—
    Triple-crowned Plinlimmon stern,
Speeds away his green haired-daughters,
    Dancing from his mossy urn:

---

[54] Cader Idris is the third highest. Idris was an astronomer. Tradition says that any one who stays a night on the top of Cader Idris will be either mad, dead, or a poet, in the morning.

[55] Arren, a very high mountain at the head of Bala Lake. The tradition here is that Arthur did not really die when he was supposed so to do, but became enchanted, at the bottom of the lake, doubtless, in some grotto, or "crystal palace," befitting his high rank.

Hoarse Clywedog—rippling Rheidol—
  Sweeping Llyfnant—witching Wye—
Severn,[56] for an outraged bridal,
  Offering vengeance all too nigh!

Oh, but thou canst efface
  That stigma, beauteous river—
Thy fair career to trace,
  Would tire a poet never:
How, from the rocky rise
  Where thou wast born,
Thou growest to fertilize,
  To strengthen, and adorn:
What cities, great and fair,
  Thy gentle windings wrap;
Till the tall forest thou dost bear,
That wafts our riches everywhere,
  Upon thine ocean lap.

These are thy glories now—
  Far other have they been—
Thy waters erst did flow
  Two adverse realms between:

---

[56] The tradition of the Severn is, that Locrinus having become enamoured of Esyllt, kept her concealed in a ship with her daughter Hafren, which being at length discovered by his wife, Gwenddolen, that high-spirited lady waged war upon him, dethroned and slew him, and victimized her rival and the daughter in the Severn, called Hafren in the British language, and Latinized into "Sabrina."

Washed round the massive foot
    Of walls that skyward towered,
And filled the guardian moat
    O'er which the drawbridge lowered.

Reflected on thy wave
    Was many a warrior's form—
It oft became their grave
    From the dread breach and storm.

Such were thy trophies—all
    Thy mediæval glory—
We would not such recall,
    But to adorn a story.

Howbeit, in thy most palmy days,
Gathers thy stream no higher praise.
Than when in tuneful calm it strays
    Through lovely Powis-land.[57]
Half to describe the varied charms
Embraced within its winding arms,
    Whole volumes would demand.

---

[57] The territorial divisions of Cymru varied at different times, like the succession. Sometimes they were all united under one chief, as Rhodri, at other times they formed three, and often more, distinct states. Powis-land included Montgomeryshire, and sometimes part of Shropshire, Denbighshire, and other adjoining counties.

Historic recollections aid
The scenic beauties here displayed,
Advancing, scarce a step is made
    Except on classic ground.
Each hill—each plain—each valley rife
With memories of the mighty strife
Of man with man, for all in life
    That's dear to man, is found.
Chief over all, in regal pride,
Where most the mountain chains divide,
And guarded strong on every side,
    Trefaldwyn's[58] castled mound.

But nothing nature's charms avail
To eyes that blinding passions scale;
The sovereign lady of the vale
    With cold distaste surveyed;
As seated in her royal bower,
Upon a lofty angle tower,

---

[58] Montgomery Castle called in the British language, Trefaldwyn, from Baldwin, Earl of Chester, its founder, temp. William the Conqueror. The whole of this district, including Plinlimmon itself, has been the scene of military activity from the time of the Romans through mediæval ages. The mountain is intersected with ancient roads, and is even thought to derive its name from "five beacons" on its summits. Carno and Caersws are both the positions of extensive military posts and momentous battles. The Breiddin hills adjacent, claim to be the site of the last battle of Caradoc, the pet Hero of British History.

The matchless landscape o'er,
    Her listless glances strayed.

In vain her damsels, skilled in art,
Some varied pastime still to start,
Might stimulate the jaded heart,
    And fill the vacant hour—
In vain the 'broidered web they spread,
In vain unwind the golden thread,
Bright through the mazy tissue led,
    In form of bird or flower.

In vain, with horn, and hawk, and hound,
And snorting steed that spurns the ground,
The sylvan train comes trooping round,
    To try her favourite sport:—
In vain the page from distant climes,
With tuneful string and storied rhymes,
That wont to please in bygone times,
    Essays her ear to court.

"Give me nor sport, nor song," she cries,
"Grant only to my longing eyes
Revenge on him who dare despise
    Their too approving look.

Lead forth, my sire, thy warlike host,
And doubly arm each frontier post,
Let not the proud despiser boast
    That I his scorn could brook!
Talk not to me of former aid,
The service of a life were paid
Too dear by aught that can degrade!"

  'T was thus the Princess spoke,
When from the oriel's mullioned bay,
Behold—the sun's descending ray
Was glittering on an armed array,
And down the slope their dashing way
    A mounted squadron took.

A snow-white pennon, like a star,
Announced that their approach from far
Was all in friendship, nought in war;
    And as they nearer drew,
The blazing sun-light soon revealed
Their fluttering banner's azure shield,
And by the dragon, vert and scaled,
    A Gwynedd Chief they knew.
With checking speed, as closer yet
The outer bastioned steep they met,
They halted at the castle gate,
    And loud their bugle blew.

Crimsoned the Princess' cheek with ire—
Flashed from her eyes a scorching fire—
" By heaven," she cried, "my just desire
   Doth fate itself fulfil!
Ye warders, sound the rallying cry—
Mount culverin and arblast high,
And archers, let your death-storm fly—
   Let every arrow kill!"

"Nay, daughter, nay," the father saith,
"It were the foulest scorn and scaith
To kingly and to knightly faith
   To meet the stranger so:[59]
The triple due of every guest
Who comes in peace—food, welcome, rest—
Concede we, and, without request,
   He shall his mission show."[60]

The sacred rites of hostship e'en
The Princess could not contravene,

---

[59] The claims of hospitality in half-civilized communities are exceeding strong, and among the Britons were peculiarly so. One of the Triads of Politeness says, (No. 19), "The three claimants of politeness:—A stranger, the performer of feats, and one who has lost his way."

[60] It was inadmissible, according to the Triads of Politeness, to ask the cause of a stranger coming; but the same code made it imperative on the stranger to announce it without being asked as soon as his host had performed his duty of reception, &c.

But heard with undisguised chagrin
   Responsive trumpets blow;
The huge portcullis' creaking chain,
The tramping of the warrior train,
As now the castle court they gain,
And all in ranks their chargers rein,
   With measured step and slow.

Advanced a horse's length apace
Were three, and he in middle place
Was still advanced an equal space
   Before the other twain :
And when from out the castle hall
The venerable seneschal
Came forth with his attendants all,
   A long and stately train,
In duteous service to the knight,
Down from their steeds the squires alight,
One holds his shield and spear of might,
   And one his bridle-rein.

Ere yet announced, no doubt could be
That he was of supreme degree,
For round his arm, and neck, and knee,
   Was clasped the golden chain :[61]

---

[61] These golden chains round the neck, arm, and knee, were peculiar to royalty. See frequent mention of them in "Enwogion." Mrs. Hemans in her "Lament of Llywarch Hên over his Sons" alludes to them.

And when the fitting moment came
His designation to proclaim,
   With Uthyr, son of Owain's name,
      The spacious court-yard rung.
The comely youths who with him rade,
In camp and court to render aid,
Becoming one of princely grade,
   Of noble lineage sprung:
Young Hwfa of Glyndwrddu[62] one;
The other, Hedd,[63] Olwynog's son,
In after years who glory won
      In Mercian cities strong—
And better far, whose memory gives
A blessed name that still survives
      His native fields among.

Repulsive to the ear and eye
Of her, that Princess fierce and high,
Was all that in the castle yard,
From her alcove, she saw and heard:

---

[62] Eldest son of Ithel, Lord of Iäl. *See* p. 40, line 25.

[63] He was head of one of the fifteen tribes. Lived at Llanfair Talhaiarn, where a moat still marks the site of his palace, and a field where he distributed his alms is called Maes Bendithion, Field of the Blessed. He was steward to Dafydd ab Owain Gwynedd, with whom Uthyr may be identified, and assisted that prince to carry fire and sword through England even to the walls of Coventry. see "Enwogion." His arms were sable, a hart argent, attired or. His posterity still enjoy some of his lands in the neighbourhood.

But more repellant yet to know
That when the feast was spread below,
The laws of hostship would require
That she should sit beside her sire :[64]
So strict were all those laws decreed,
That nought their force might supersede.
With haughty calm, but princely port,
She took the place assigned at court.
Beside her father on the right,
And on his left the stranger knight.

Not unobserved by Uthyr keen,
Nor unresented, was her mien;
But he resolved to work his ends,
And then exact severe amends
For all the pangs that love and pride
Inflict, when they the soul divide.

His outward bearing now was all
That best befits a princely hall;
And, ere the Princess had fulfilled
Her irksome task, had partly stilled

---

[64] The Thirty-fourth Triad of Politeness says,—Three persons whom the host should make to partake of food and friendship with his guests— his wife, his eldest son, and his eldest daughter, which ever of them he may happen to have; and he himself superintending.

The angry throbbings of her breast
Towards such a young and courtly guest:
So that she heard with less disdain,
When rising with her damsel train
To quit the hall, his humble boon
For audience on the morrow's noon.
Her sire's approof the suit sustained,
Which Uthyr had to him explained:
For Grüffydd, generous and wise,
Rejoiced that with his old allies
A better footing might be won,
E'en on a step below the throne;
And heard, with condescending grace,
The prayer that Uthyr might replace
Young Madog in that envied rank
From which he had so strangely shrank.

Not so the Princess—here his task
Would a far harder effort ask;
And test to the extremest strain,
His daring front and subtle brain.
Her look the suitor might have scared,
Who more had scrupled—less had dared,
When first his purpose he declared.
And haughty scoffs, or pouting spleen,
Broke in his tempered words between.

But as he soon contrived to hinge
On his ambitions her revenge,
A more attentive ear she lent,
Her lip uncurled—her brow unbent:
Of Madog's wreck she hailed the thought,
Though with her own insanely bought;
And linked herself with one abhorred,
To ruin him her soul adored.

In wily phrase he forward set
The public scorn her charms had met:
Charms which alone might compensate
For loss of heritage and state,
And yet accompanied by both,
Had found reception chill and loth.
What mad perversion—desperate views,
Could move such chances to refuse!

A shiver shot athwart her frame—
Her breathing stopped—then quicker came—
Her speech, which seemed awhile to choke,
Into long whispers hissing broke.

"It is—it must—I see it all—
Some passion doth his heart enthral—
Some upstart minion—witching fool,
Holds base dominion o'er his soul.

Now mark me—this must be the first
Just sacrifice to vengeance' thirst—
Forbear reply—it matters nought
How far—how long—how dearly sought—
To me the victim must be brought.
Haunt his existence—dog his feet—
Shroud him no darkness—no retreat—
Till his base secret sees the day,
And my deep wrongs are wiped away!"

"August Princess, but less august
Than beautiful, your wrath is just,
And I a slave to do your trust.
But granted that the wretch you mean
Exists, she cannot intervene
To mar our rights, but rather aid:
Since Madog, thus obscurely wed,
Would shake his claim to kingly powers,
And what shakes his must strengthen ours."

With lip in bitter smile compressed
The Princess heard—" Sir Prince, you jest,
You dream—forget—or never knew
The blood these veins that courses through—

Have never heard of Owain's[65] name
Who kindled Dyfed[66] into flame
Ere he would banish from his breast
The image of the beauteous Nêst;
By whose yet unseen charms inspired,
He Pembroke's lordly castle fired,
And Norman shaft and lance defied,
And bore away De Windsor's bride.
Such was his love—is his revenge
A theme in Cymru new and strange?
Was it in covert or disguise
He quenched the light of Madog's eyes?"

Scoffing she spake, and scoffing smiled;
And even Uthyr half recoiled.

" For me to see your brother wed
And live, are notions that agree
  Like flaming ice, or floating lead—

---

[65] This was Owain ab Cadwgan, Prince of Powis, who, hearing the beauty of Nêst, the wife of Gerald De Windsor, Constable of Pembroke Castle, extolled at a feast given by his father at Cardigan, resolved to carry her off, and effected that object by setting fire to the Castle. Some years after, however, he was slain by the said Constable. Owain's revenge was on Madog ab Rhirid, for the murder of Cadwgan, at Pool; he put his eyes out. *See* "Enwogion Cymru," for all these particulars, *in vocibus* Owain, and Madog.

[66] Dyfed, Pembrokeshire

Incongruous things that cannot be—
So find the Idol out, and bring to me."

"Great Princess, be it so—yet deign
My humble suit meantime to list—
  To wait her death were surely vain
Who yet we know not doth exist.
The King sinks fast—the crisis may be missed."

The Princess paused a moment's space.
With brow intent—" There is a place
  In Meirion's desert drear,
A triple-sided altar lone,
And to a question on that stone,
Traced with the blood that heirs a throne,
  True answer thou shalt hear.
This know I from an aged nurse.
Who, dying, bound me with a curse
  The secret ne'er to try
But once, and that in such a strait
As on the issue should my fate
  Depend—to live or die.
That strait is come—my life involved
In having these my doubts resolved;
Born to a throne, lo, thus I shed

The blood to which the voices dread
   Of occult POWERS reply ! "

So saying from her 'broidered zone
   A tiny blade she drew,
Whose hilt with dazzling diamonds shone,
   And edge was tempered true;
And ere the Prince could interpose,
   Had pierced her ivory arm,
And, as the ruddy fountain rose,
She snatched a phial to enclose,
   In crystal tube, the charm.

" Take this," she said, " and go thy way
To Llwyn Saint, without delay ;
Inscribe the stone at twilight grey,
And wait THE VOICE till dawn of day."

'T was plain the Princess would allow
No further parley—why, or how—
And therefore, with obeisance low,
   He took the sacred charge ;
And on her wisdom, power, and beauty,
And his deep reverence and duty,
   Did fittingly enlarge.

To all of this the Princess lent
A deafened ear, for wholly bent
Was she upon the deep portent,
   And vengeance dire to wreak ;
With courtesy that rose not higher
Than scant what triads would require,
Was Uthyr motioned to retire,
   Nor suffered more to speak.
But he could bear the transient rule
Of one whom passion made his tool,
   And judgment blind and weak.

Next day, all interchanges meet
   Of host and guest, with Grüffydd o'er,
The Gwynedd Prince, his squires and suite,
   Rode forth in order as before.

But when they reached the river plain,
   Where branching tracks the way divide,
In Hwfa's charge he left his train,
   Westward with Hedd alone to ride.

'T were gain if there were time to dwell
   On every step that marked their way,
Rock, plain, and river—hill and dell—
   Tower, town, cot, hamlet—" fair Abbaye."

Caereinion's timber bulwarks, built
    By Madog ab Meredydd, where
Had Powis blood by hands been spilt
    That in that princely blood did share.[67]

The spreading vale where Madog's bier,
    After its long death-march, reposed,
From Winton, where his strange career,[68]
    In foreign land, as strangely closed.

The meads where Tanat, o'er the green,
    Unwinds his azure silken skein;
The rugged passes which between
    Is breasted Berwyn's alpine chain.

High on the right that purple peak
    Which memories the royal fair,[69]
The insult on whose gentle cheek
    Whole massacres could not repair.

---

[67] Iorwerth ab Bleddyn, a Prince of Powis, soon after his release from a long imprisonment in which he had been kept by Henry I. of England, was treacherously murdered at Caereinion, by his nephew, Madog ab Rhirid, who also slew Cadwgan. *See* note 65, p. 109.

[68] He had sided with Henry II. in his first attack on Wales. He resided much in England, and died at Winchester, whence his body was brought to Meifod for burial. Powell says of him, "He was ever the King of England's friend, and was one that feared God, and relieved the poor." The former praise is rather ambiguous in the mouth of a Cymro.

[69] Bronwen, the daughter of Llyr, sister of Brân, and wife of Matholwch, a King of Ireland, is recorded in the Triads as having

But Uthyr passed without a thought
　The injured Bronwen's lofty rest;
His crafty mind was wholly fraught
　With Erffraid's wild and dark behest.

Why should he waste the wondrous spell
　In gaining knowledge of a fact
The which to change would not avail
　His schemes, but rather counteract?

'T were best procure a substitute
　To satisfy the Princess' hate,
And with the charm a question put
　Should bear upon his future fate.

Thus weighing deep and sifting through
　The chances of his felon plot,
As night her veil o'er nature drew,
　The Prince approached the fated spot,

---

suffered a blow which, from its results, was called "one of the three fatal blows of the Isle of Britain;" namely a box on the ear from her husband Matholwch, to avenge which her brother, Brân, "half depopulated" Ireland. Mr. Fitzroy, the mover of the "Aggravated Assaults' Bill" lately brought before Parliament, could scarce wish a more summary way of proceeding than this. For the substance of these four last notes, *vide* Mr. Williams's "Enwogion."

And wrote upon the altar stone
" SHALL UTHYR REIGN ON GWYNEDD'S THRONE?"
Then summoned patience to await,
Till dawn of day, the voice of Fate.

But destiny had not decreed
The march of things should thus proceed—
Scarce had he traced the final word,
When, from another cell, he heard
A voice familiar to his ear—
It was the King's impassioned prayer—
And then the answer—"NEVER!"—low but clear.

" What," cried the Prince, below his breath,
" Answered so soon—yet by my faith,
That little voice, so soft and sweet,
Sounds not to me like that of Fate—
But rather that far better known
In daily dealings—woman's tone :
In spite of spirit, saint, and spell,
I will explore the neighbour cell.
Should the result be as I guess
The case may meet my present stress,
And a fair sacrifice supply
The Princess' spite to satisfy.

By Ellyll, she deserves to die,[70]
Who has given me that thwart reply."

So saying, through the leafy shade
That screened the altar's deep arcade,
With step so stealthy did he glide,
As to attain the other side
Without occasioning alarm,
  And by the fading light discerned,
Upon the earth, a female form
  On bended knee, with face upturned.

Something there was, or in the grace
That clothed that form, or in the place,
That staggered Uthyr's onward pace.
  And fixed him to the spot:
Nor while the king continued near
Would it be wise the maid to scare—
He stood aside, till from her prayer
  She rose, and left the grot.

As forth she tottered he perceived
Some powerful emotion heaved

---

[70] Ellyll, a chief dæmon of Druid Mythology; it had some *aliases* as "Andras," and "Malen."

Her slender form—some steps she made,
Then paused, and on her drooping head
Pressed tight her hands, while broken sobs
Were struggling 'neath her bosom's throbs.

Still Uthyr lingered—" Some distress
Disturbs our little Pythoness—
'T is hard—so young and fair—but yet
Such only can the purpose fit—
Ugly and old, 't were little use,
As Erffraid's rival, to produce."

Thus arguing, forth with rapid tread
He stepped, and stood before the maid,
Who shrieked, recoiled, and would have fled;
But Uthyr stopped with quiet force,
And deep salute, her forward course—
" Whence, lovely Prophet, this alarm?
To ward, and not occasion harm,
Are manly sword and manly arm—
It is not meet that one so slight
And young should roam alone at night."

This forced emollient failed to soothe
The agitated girl—in truth

Her spirit more bewildered seemed
Accosted thus—and loud she screamed.

And now an echoing voice was heard;
And soon a bounding footstep neared;
And through the dusk a form appeared.
"What, ho!—distress—a woman's cry!—
A call true knight can ne'er deny—
Again adventure must be nigh!"

"'T is jingling Hywel—by the death,"
Said Uthyr through his grinding teeth,
"Pert fool, to stumble in my way!"
And then aloud, "Fair brother, nay,
No woman this, but witch, or fay,
Who gives, or feigns to give, divine
Responses at the mystic shrine:
But now to Owain, in the cave,
Oracular reply she gave:
For this, in strictness, there were need
At Caerlleon's synod she should plead."

"Brother of mine, this stretch of zeal,
For churchly privilege and weal,
Of churchmen grave may gain applause—
Enough for me are knighthood's laws,
Which bind me fast to woman's cause;

And be she witch or what she will,
Her champion I through good and ill."

"Sir Harper, pray you, pitch your key
Less sharply when you speak to me.
I ne'er aspired to go to school
To you for knightly code and rule.
For errant knight like you a dame
As errant, perhaps, is fitting game;
But I have here a graver claim
Yet, though I ask not your permit
T' assign the dame as I see fit,
I said not that I *should*, but might,
In strictness, plead the Church's right
To guard the limits of the faith—
But lo, a voice—we're joined—'t is Hedd."[71]

It was that sage and faithful squire,
Who heard the sounds of rising ire,
From where he did his lord await;
And now, to stay the sharp debate,
With prudent counsel intervened,
(Which all conflicting views amened),
That to the judgment of the King,
So near abiding, they should bring

---

[71] Pronounced "Heth."

The damsel straightway, and his high
Award the question satisfy.
Not far remote the royal tent
Was pitched till day—to that they went:
The girl by gentler words in part
Assured, but still with fluttering heart,
By Hedd in courteous guidance ta'en,
And followed by the chafing twain.

Before the royal presence dread
The fair accused was promptly led;
And what the dusk had erst concealed,
The blazing torches now revealed—
Her touching beauty, grace, and youth—
Reproach of guilt, but sense of truth.

A feeling murmured through the throng—
Such looks they could not join with wrong ·
Kindled the monarch's faded eye ;
And almost Hywel bent the knee :
E'en Uthyr, 'spite his " triple brass,"
Wished he had let the adventure pass.
But with his credit now at stake,
Need was presentment he should make.
And as the King's Confessor stood
At hand, he hoped in sterner mood
By him the matter might be viewed.

Something of sorcery he spake—
The tonsured head began to shake—
Of sacrilege—a dreaded word,
And treason, too, was something heard—
To blink a king with words of fate
But false, was sure a crime of state!

" And was it thus," exclaimed the king,
  " Was this the granter of my prayer?
Has dæmon, witch, or evil thing
  A voice so sweet—a form so fair?
To tell a prince's doom how didst thou dare,
If that thou art of earth, and not of air?"

  A moment's pause—her shrinking form,
The woman raised, and bending head,
  As doth the lily when the storm
    Its rigours all hath shed,
    And left it bruised, not dead.

She looked at Owain—in his eye
  She seemed to read of mercy—then
With firmer step and look, drew nigh,
  Dropped on her knees, and thus began:—

Great King, I am attainted here
   Of solemn charges, deep offence ;
Yet is my inward conscience clear
   Of sacrilegious, vain pretence.
Thus humbly do I urge my weak defence.
If with rash seeming to your pious prayer
I answer made, it was not idle prate,
Nor bold assumption of the powers of fate.

That Madog ne'er shall sacrifice
   His throne and bride of high degree,
And wed the maiden of his choice,
   I can pronounce, for—I am S<small>HE</small> !

And thus his vows and plighted troth,
   My present joy and future hope,
I cancel, and, by every oath
   That binds on earth, do render up ! "

Through present awe and future dread,
Through terrors pending—pleasures fled—
A halo circled round the maid
   Of majesty and calm :
The deep impassioned energies
That did with the emergence rise,

Wound up her powers, and o'er her eyes
   She pressed her slender palm.

While through the minds of those around
   The various thoughts that passed before
Seemed now, sole wonder, to confound,
   All other feeling surging o'er.

But further as the King desired
   Of this mysterious thing to know.
All but the maid and monk retired—
   The King's compassion willed it so.

Then poured the damsel forth her tale,
   Ingenuous from her guileless breast;
So as the hardest scarce could fail
   With all its truth to be impressed.

Conviction touched the royal mind,
   And had he been alone to act.
The King would never have inclined
   A further surety to exact.

And would have left her broken heart
   Within her humble home to find
The consolation which in part
   Waits ever on the upright mind.

But then began to interpose,
  The holy father, and to urge,
"That best the maid would find repose
  Within a convent's peaceful verge.

A generous impulse doubtless moved
  Her now, but how could they rely,
That importuned by one she loved,
  She would continue to deny?

To Llangwm's tribute cell that eve
  Himself the novice would convey,
And there in sure protection leave,
  For furtherance on a future day.

'T were best affix the church's seal
  That she renounce the world and man,
To tend her soul's immortal weal,
  Among the Sisters of Maenan."

The girl, bewildered and depressed—
  The king, dejected and amazed—
In all this bidding acquiesed,
  Without a doubt or murmur raised.

A PRINCE OF WALES
LONG AGO

CANIAD SIXTH.

CANIAD VI.

I WALKED in the forest when autumn was closing,
  When winds through its half-unroofed corridores sigh,
Deep and omened, like dreams of a hero reposing,
  When triumphs are finished and dangers are nigh.

The trophies of summer were everywhere scattered—
  The wreaths of his glory were trampled and sere—
On those still remaining the heavy drops pattered,
  And told that the trials of winter were near.

To my fancy it seemed that, like sentient creatures,
  The trees of the wood in this crisis displayed
The moods that distinguish intelligent natures,
  As, fortitude—meekness—intelligence—dread.

The aspen was voiceless—his hair wildly bristled—
  As 'waiting the stroke of some terrible doom—
Thro' the ash's pale tresses the hollow winds whistled—
  The arms of the cypress were folded in gloom.

But, tranquil, an oak in the midst was outspreading
   His masses of shadow, scarce thinned by the blast.
At whose touch his less steadfast companions were
      shedding,
   With panic profusion, the pride of the past.

I paused to contemplate an emblem suggesting
   So much of the noble, pathetic, and true—
An object of sense so majestic investing
   The deep hidden things with a form and a hue.

His root with the globe's solid frame-work was twisted,
   His shaft seemed a pillar supporting the skies;
'T was as if his expanse had with theirs co-existed,
   Fair twins in conception, creation, and rise!

It was hard to believe that an object so stately,
   Of bulk so stupendous, and measure so vast,
Had sprung from the earth in comparison lately,
   Or a term less longœval was destined to last!

The while deep'ning thoughts were my fancy absorbing,
   Through the thickening layers of the high tufty shade,
Came a small tapping sound, the green silence dis-
      turbing,
   And on the crisp carpet a soft rustling made.

'T was an acorn, full ripe, that some while had awaited
    The touch of a zephyr, its signal to fall,
And work out the purpose for which 't was created—
    An end how prodigious—beginning how small!

From a cup scarce sufficing to brim for a revel,
    At Oberon's wedding, for Puck and the fays,
Flows a fount branching wider, and passing the level
    Of jets made to pamper a Sybarite's gaze.

And thus arise families—dynasties—nations—
    The chain of events and the crises of states—
Convulsions that rock the earth's solid foundations,
    A spark, chance-ignited, for havoc completes.

All silent and slow in the workshops of nature,
    For years, or for ages, uniting at length,
The powers of strife, overflowing their crater,
    Put forth in an instant their horrible strength.

And thus in the bosom of man, as a furnace,
    When elements baleful are left to combine,
They burst as the boilings from fabled Avernus,
    And roll the red ruin in pathways malign.

And thus was the leaven of malice fermenting
  In Gwynedd, my country, the hapless—the fair—
Attuned to the theme is the voice of lamenting,
  That floats o'er the waters, and thrills on the air.

Hush the soft waves on a shore sweeter smiling—
  Smiles there a shore upon waves more serene
Than where a bright belt girds that beautiful isle in—
  Where Menai the golden laps Mona the green?

Is there a trait of the beautiful wanting—
  Lacks there a feature of vast or sublime?—
Vallies that ring as with welcomes enchanting—
  Mountains that send forth the echoes of time.

But now every sound of enjoyment is failing—
  For the voices of nature from man's take their tone,
And over Malltraeth comes the key-note of wailing,
  And distant Diganwy responds to the moan.

   Mourn for the mighty laid low—
     The hero of a hundred fields—
     The conqueror of conquerors yields—
   Yields to one only foe!

His sword that knew no sheath
While an enemy had breath,
Could deal the doom of death,
    But not avert its blow!

Weep for the Father-King—
Cymru your tribute bring—
Wreaths of dark ivy fling—
    Emblem of woe!
With it the heath entwine,
Showing that, still divine,
High among stars to shine,
    His soul shall go.

Mourn him then not as lost—
His spirit o'er the host
    Ever shall fly.
Still shall his glorious name
Light up the path of fame—
Heroes may leave us, but never can die!

Such were the notes that rose and fell
As Arfon's breezes caught the knell,
And bore its sadness on the air,
For the far wilderness to share.

Deep answered deep—shore answered shore—
Timed meetly to the muffled oar,
Whose solemn beat was multiplied
A thousand-fold, as o'er the tide
  A funeral pomp they bore.

Barge followed barge, at distance due—
With ensigns of funereal hue,
That sadly drooping from their staves,
Mingled their weeping with the wave's.

High in the midst a dark gondole,
Whose trophied pride veiled Christian dole,
Bore on its deck a coffin-bed,
Whereon a royal corpse was laid,
With regal trappings—sceptred palm,
In posture as of slumber calm,
With upturned look through curtained eyes,
As if in dreams it sought the skies.

'T was OWAIN THE VALIANT borne home to his rest,
Beside the sea-river, in Bangor the Blest.

  Soon as the galley touched the strand
    A chosen warrior train drew near,
  Lifted the couch with reverent hand,
    And laid it on a stately bier.

Then their thrice " honourable load "
  Devoutly on their shoulders raise,
And bear it to its last abode,
  With tears of sorrow—songs of praise—

The massive *cist*, whose sculptured lid
  Presents the monarch's effigy,
Beneath the marble pavement hid,
  Before the altar high.

And as they neared the sacred fane,
There met them many a holy train—
Each abbey, convent, spital, cell,
Sent forth deputed bands to swell
The last ovation of their king,
And incense burn, and requiems sing.

Three solemn days turned into night,
With windows veiled and torches' light,
That hallowed form lay in the sight
  Of great and small to view:
That to a king, as father dear,
Each might with reverence draw near,
  And take a last adieu.

The watches changed, but each relief
Was headed by a Gwynedd Chief
Of knightly tribe, the five-and-ten—[72]
The noblest races' noblest men—
The bulwarks proud of Gwynedd's throne:
But with these watchers there was one
Who quitted not—the royal son—
Whose duteous hand had been the stay
Of his great sire's declining day,
Now tended with untiring eyes,
By day and night, his obsequies.

At length the corpse, all honours paid,
Within the sculptured cist was laid.

It was the Prince's duty now
To lift from off the royal brow
The kingly crown, and from the hand
To gently take the sceptre wand;
No meaner touch might dare invade
The precincts of the sacred shade,
And when that youthful form bent down,
And touch so soft removed the crown

---

[72] The "fifteen tribes," so often alluded to, were the elite of Gwynedd Nobility; corresponding to the Florentine "Trecenti," and similar mediæval grades all over Europe

That scarce the cushion, edged with gold,
Beneath the head was changed in fold,
The thousands who the minster filled,
With voice, attention, breathing stilled—
Bethought them of the counter-scene
Which late their congress did convene,
To see the sire at Maesmawr's mound
Crowning the son—now by that son uncrowned!

But while the glittering toy he held,
Far other thoughts his bosom swelled
Than pride to feel it touch his brow,
On which to set it waited now
A mitred bishop, for the laws
Of Cymru could not brook a pause—
A kingless space between two reigns—
But still the Prince's thoughts enchains
His father's well known, much loved face,
Which kept in death the matchless grace
That had in life devotion won
From all, and most that darling son.

The spacious vault with life that teemed,
And yet so still that more it seemed

A pictured scene—the dazzling light—
One noiseless minute—made a sight
Ne'er seen before——but while, within,
The dome had echoed to a pin,
Without arose a gathering sound
That strangely broke the calm profound,
And mixing soon with vague alarms,
Arose the cry, " To arms! to arms! "

Close at the Minster's massive door
Was raging now a tumult's roar—
Confusion spread—the rites were stopped,
And, omen dire! the bishop dropped
The crown or e'er it touched the head
Of Madog, who had forward sped
The cause of the affray to learn,
Make tumult cease, and peace return.
Unarmed, and clad in garb of woe,
He flew to see what sudden foe
Or uproar rash should intervene
To mar his life's most solemn scene.

Through terror's and amazement's storm,
The rumours now assumed a form:

And thus it was—a warlike band,
'Neath standards of the Powis-land
With Uthyr in supreme command,
And joined to him his Powis wife
Came on, prepared for utmost strife.

So deeply planned by aid of spies,
They brought to bear this dread surprise,
When all unarmed and drowned in grief,
Scarce Gwynedd had or king or chief—
It seemed as if her strength was all
Enclosed within that minster wall,
And that the glories of her head
At one fell blow might now be shed.

Correctly to describe were vain
What consternation filled the fane.
E'en warlike thousands there arrayed,
To grace the pageant, felt dismayed
At such a sudden ambuscade.
What then the wilderment and dread
Among the feebler crowds that spread—
The troops of holy men who swelled
The pomp; and holy maids, who filled
High galleries faced with lattice wires,
And youths arranged in tuneful choirs!

What words—what colours, could convey.
An image of that wild affray?

Among the bold and wise, who lead
In such-like straits, what headlong rede—
What various counsel—steps how rash
The maze involve—increase the crash.

And more than all—what wrath—what dole—
What dire revulsion of the soul
Pierced Madog through—what bitter smart
Tore up his nerves, and flesh, and heart!
That heart with filial anguish rent,
That soul on filial duty bent,
Dragged into violence and hate
Ere yet those duties were complete—
Snatched from his father's closing grave,
'Mid yelling hordes to clash and rave.

    Yet now, when all the truth,
  Of sacrilege, and treason's guilt,
  Of blood in torrents to be spilt,
  Flashed out—on basis surely built
    Stood forth the god-like youth.

.

A minute's thought showed all the strait—
A brief command to chiefs of weight
He gave, to guard each outer gate—
   A gentle word to soothe
Of weaker sort and sex the fear—
A dauntless voice and eye, to cheer
The brave—a heart each risk to share
   And every peril smooth.

But most of all he did insist
With limb and life to guard the cist,
And every effort to resist
   That on it should be made—
The chief behest to Iorwerth gave—
In valour equal—next in grade—
   To watch their father's grave.

Such rapid dispositions now
As such emergence would allow,
Completed in the church below,
   Up to the battled roof
Young Madog mounted, in the hope
A parley with the foe to ope
From thence, 'whose bearing, drift and scope,
   Should meet e'en his approof.

There, looking from a turret high,
A sight repulsive met his eye—
Aggressive swarms that occupy
    The territory round:
And more repulsive still the sight—
A traitor brother—recreant knight,
And dame whom passions vile incite,
    Their leaders base are found.

The Princess on a steed of might,
With golden housings richly dight,
Such as bore Büddig[73] to the fight,
    Stood on a 'vantage ground:
Her dear-bought husband, on her right,
Appeared some orders to indite
To squires, and looked not easy quite,
    Nor moved his eyes around;
When Madog from the minster wall
Summoned them by a trumpet's call,
With him in love and friendship all
    In conference to unite.

What meant, he asked, that armed array—
That rude approach—that wild affray,
And that on such a solemn day

[73] Boadicea.

From kindred to their kin?
As brother and as sister, he
Right glad to welcome them should be,
Came they in peace and amity,
   His home and heart within.

But was it fitting to appear
A father's closing tomb so near
And his departing shade to scare,
   With war's unhallowed din?
Disband they, then, that hostile horde,
The trumpet silence, sheathe the sword,
Stretch forth the arms of sweet accord,
   And peaceful triumphs win!

The consort pair while thus addressed,
Gave signs that variously impressed
Thereby were they—with lip compressed,
   The princess heard, and flashing eye:
And many a sound of scorn suppressed,
And many a move of hot unrest
She made, as to the grave behest
   'Gan Uthyr make reply.

He heard with look unmoved, but stern,
That did nor this nor that way turn—
Then said, "Sir Prince, if thou wouldst learn

Of our approach the why,
I would advise you recollect
That when your forehead was bedecked
By our great sire, he did connect
    With that distinction high
Another main condition ere
That band should make you Gwynedd's heir,
Which was to wed this royal fair,
    And that, Sir Prince, have I !
Which being so, it now remains
That she and 1 to our domains,
And all that here-ways appertains
    To paramount degree,
Do straight succeed and rise—and then,
Dispersed this appareil of men,
Accept your subject homage when.
    You bend the duteous knee."

A flush enkindled Madog's brow—
It passed—" No time to bandy now
Hard words—A truce that may allow
    The sacred pending rite
In safe decorum to complete,
I ask—and questions then will treat
Referring to our royal seat,
    And ward the threatened fight—

As surety for the truce ye twain
Within the precincts of the fane.
To join the royal funeral train
   I solemnly invite.
If there your safety I infringe,
This army shall your fate avenge—
If they assault these holy towers,
Your safety then shall purchase ours."

" 'T is well," 'gan Uthyr—but the word
Arrested was or e'er 't was heard,
But by the Princess, who in haste
Upon her lip her finger placed—
" How now?" she cried, below her breath.
" No truce will serve, I swore his death,
Or mine—or both—" " Nay, nay," he cried,
In tones the like. " be satisfied—
All will be as you list—" Then high
To Madog slowly made reply
While on the gates was fixed his eye—

" So be it—fits it well to grace
Our predecessor's resting place—
With presence of—ourself—and—bride—
So let—the portals—open—wide—"

L

The Prince rejoined, " That word I go
To give, which none else dare, below—
But, how is this—now, by the souls
Of all my sires,—the gate unrolls
Its ponderous hinge—and thereward tend
The Powis hordes—quick—quick—descend—
There 's treason Rhirid !" to his aide,
" Whoe'er the traitor. we 're betrayed!"
Now down the stair that winding leads
From the high roof, he flying treads,
While Rhirid close its mazes thrids

As through the steepy dusk he flies,
The sounds of gathering tumult rise :
Within the lofty pile—without—
Command—reproach—wild scream and shout
The crash of onslaught—struggle—rout—
And mixed with man's, in jarring key,
Shrill tones of woman's agony.

It seemed a maddening age before
He reached the staircase entrance door—
Emerging from its narrow vault,
How did the scene his soul revolt !

Custom ordained that who in chief
At funeral mourned, in proof of grief,
No sort of weapon should retain,
Or hand, or dress within—not e'en
The sharp but slender girdle blade,
That times unsettled needful made :
Thus helpless through that dire mêlée
He had to make his fearful way,
Where now did such confusion grow
That friend could scarce be known from foe ;
Behind him close, or at his side,
With whirling sword and iron stride,
Did Rhirid all perform to guard,
That could, his dear and sovereign lord.
The thought that Madog's mind engrossed
Was not a princedom won or lost,
But his great father's honoured grave
From desecration dire to save.
That was his goal of duteous love
That-ward his perilled path he clove.
Each step he made, a scene of new
And desperate strife became, as through
Now hostile contact—friendly now,
And still unscathed, he knew not how,
He onward pressed—young Rhirid's arm
Still staving off impending harm.

Now, when their struggling progress brought
Their steps to where most hotly fought
The foes who through the abbey door,
Their yelling masses thickening pour.
With those who, loyal but perplexed,
'Mongst rebels in the aisles were mixed,
Above the surging crowds were seen
The heads of Uthyr and his queen.
And, now convict, their traitor guide,
The swarthy Ithel[74] by their side.

A pang of indignation shot
Through Madog, but he tarried not
To breathe it forth—his soul intent—
His every effort, to prevent
The desecration of the grave,
From carnage raging in the nave.
" On, Rhirid, on—by heaven and all
Therein, the recreant Lord of Iäl
Now shows, with high exulting hand,
The spot to which his perjured band
Their course pursue—the altar's pale
Their myrmidons prepare to scale—

---

[74] Ithel, Lord of Iäl, surnamed, y Velyn, the swarthy.

To intercept their vile approach
And save my own life-long reproach,
No way remains—no chance—no time,
But o'er this marble mass to climb—
My grandsire's sculptured cenotaph—
So cut their dire approaches off!"

An anxious observation glanced
Young Rhirid upward—high advanced,
Ab Cynan's monumental pile
Stood out from the receding aisle,
And o'er its steep and polished height,
With shapes and shields and trophies dight,
A shorter, but imperilled, way,
To gain the altar precincts lay.

He shuddered—but or e'er his tongue
Could frame a doubt, young Madog swung,
Upstepping from the shoulders strong
Of those near standing—thence to spring
Upon some hero's form—thence cling
Suspended from an angel's wing,
The salient angles of the tomb,
That saved him from impending doom.

Throughout the Minster far and near,
Did Madog's daring move appear,
And audible above the rout,
One loud and universal shout,
Of friends' enthusiasm rose,
And admiration e'en of foes.

   While thus suspended by a thread
      His life in balance hung,
Happed all for which his soul in faith
Had dared the fellest form of death
      The combatants among.

   All tracked in blood their course,
      The altar's pale to force.
The sacrilegious traitors fell—
     E'en Iorwerth's stalwart hand,
     Who with a loyal band,
    That last entrenchment manned,
Could not maintain the citadel.

   Bearing down every side,
     The overwhelming tide
Of men prepared and weaponed make their way,
   And now the blood-stained bride
   And perjured brother 'spied
The cist and crown within their reach that lay.

Still where the bishop down
　　　Had dropped it, lay the crown—
　Across the cist, to snatch the glittering prize,
　　　'Gan Uthyr forward stride,
　　　When, on the other side,
　Stood Madog, as descended from the skies!
　　　Then, as with an effect
　　　Of more than earth, was checked,
　By his unsworded hand, the felon's rise—
　　　Down shuddering, though unmaimed,
　　　The dastard shrunk—when gleamed
　　　A tiny poniard, aimed
　By a white female arm, and 'thwart the cist,
　　　As with a tiger's dart,
　　　The Princess at the heart
　Of Madog made a spring, which, though it missed
　　　Thus far her dark revenge,
　　　Yet by a fate more strange
　　　Accomplished it in part—
　　　Scarce by the Prince was seen
　　　The flash, when lo, between
　　　His bosom and the foe,
　　　Against the fatal blow,
　　　A living shield—and low
　Upon the coffin sunk—her gentle breath
Soft sobbing forth—a nun received the destined death!

There happen in the times of men
A kind of mental solstice, when
Upon their dial seems the ray
That marks them to decline or stay.

Such was the strange suspension now
   That in the minster's thousands seemed
To follow on that hazard blow—
   'T was as they frozen were, or dreamed.

The picture was of wondrous sort,
   The brush or chisel to inspire,
And more the fancy wild to court
   Of those who wake the living lyre—

Beside the aged sometime dead,
   A quivering prostrate female form,
From whose fair face not yet were fled
   Of youthful life the colours warm.

The Prince, although erect in life
   He stood, was pale and still as they
Who rescued now from worldly strife—
   Things of the past—before him lay!

He paused a space, and pausing felt
   An ice-bolt shiver through his frame—
Before his eyes, as down he knelt
   Beside his dead, a blackness came.

It passed, and then her marbling hand
   Within his death-like palms he took,
Unbound her virgin forehead band,
   And gave one agonizing look.

It was his Gwendda—from her breast
   The dagger dropped that saved his own—
Once more he leaned her there to rest
   That long had been her earthly throne;
   Ah me, for evermore to be alone!

To bear her from the scene he turned,
   But as he made his sad retreat,
Unwitting in his path he spurned,
   The crown that rolled beneath his feet,
   Which minded him of this announcement meet—

On Rhirid and the nuns devolved
   The precious charge's further care,
And what his mighty soul resolved
   Did Madog calmly then declare.

First to the bishop, from the nook
   Emerged, which he for safety sought,
He signed, who from the pavement took
   The glittering toy so dearly bought,

Then lifting off the slender band
His own pale brow that lightly spanned,
He placed it in the Bishop's hand,
Beside the statelier jewelled gaud,
Before the throng now over-awed,
Then in a silence deep and dread
These words of solemn import said—

" Whatever share in all this wrong—
This treason, sacrilege, and gore—
To my pretensions may belong,
Or claims, or rights, I do deplore.

In presence of the honoured dead,
And guiltless blood so rashly shed,
These proud insignia here at once,
I now and evermore renounce.

And now of every oath and pact,
   Allegiance sworn and love unbought,
This last and only proof exact—
   To stay this sacrilegious rout.

The duty we conjointly owe
  To our great father let us pay,
And after to our country show
  His life-work was not thrown away.

Shall we subvert his generous toils,
  And desolate the land again
With fury of intestine broils?
  Forbid it all that makes us men!

All selfish wishes merge we now—
  The future hail—the past forget,
And on Llywellin's[75] youthful brow
  The symbol of dominion set!"

---

[75] Llywellin, afterwards surnamed The Great, son of Iorwerth Drwyndwm; this young prince, after the troubles caused by the sons of Owain had been quelled, succeeded to the Gwynedd sovereignty, and reigned many years.

CONCLUSION.

The seasons of the year—the day's
Revolving hours—the cycling rays
That part the world-wide scope around,
With deep analogies abound :
The ruddy morn—the dancing spring,
Of youth and hope the image bring ;
The lengthened shadows of the west
Man's downward progress may suggest,
When haply o'er his visions bright
Of love, and hope, and daring flight,
Hath left its trace, the withering blight
Of disappointment, and his day
Is merging into twilight grey.

So harmonized the outer world
When, with their wing-like sails unfurled,
And anchors heaving to the song
Whose measure makes the effort strong,

A squadron in the offing lay
Of "Ceredigion's treach'rous bay,"
While a light shallop from the shore
The last for embarkation bore—
Such lingerers as ever part
From home and kin with faltering heart;
For e'en among the manlier sort
Who quit for brave achief their port,
Who elemental fury brave—
The whirling wind and whelming wave—
A double thought divides the mind
Of hope before and grief behind.
Nor were less keenly—deeply felt
These rending throbs beneath the belt
Whose broidered breadth the bosom spanned
Of him who led the daring band,
Whom to embark, the sole delay
Was now to their adventurous way.

Theirs was no every day emprise,
Which pleasure prompts or traffic hies;
No gainful cruize from mart to mart,
With depths explored and measured chart;
No legal piracy, in name
Of nation's rights to seize the game.

'T was nought of this—the exile band,
Self banished from their native land,
In duty to their god-like chief.
Were strangely working its relief.
For this was MADOG—years had past
Since he had nobly from him cast
All high ambitions, young desires
Upon his father's funeral fires,
Save one—his country's cause to serve
With every thought and every nerve ;
And thus to fill his lonely heart,
And soothe, though never cure its smart.

To prop Llywellin's reign became
His dear—his sole—his generous aim ;
And every noble sacrifice
He made the effort to suffice.
But scarcely had the crown been placed
Upon the infant brow that graced
That gift so well in age matured,
Than out the flames of discord poured.
With Uthyr still the kindling brand,
And more the fatal furnace fanned
By passions of the haughty dame
Whose love and hate alike were flame.

Each into each the other fused,
As turnfully were both aroused.
Her arm outstretched to stab or fold
As haply love or hate controlled.

From hopeless moils his soul that jarred,
And all his upright purpose marred.
In anger less than grief he bent
His mind at length to this intent—
The watery waste to traverse o'er,
Its unknown distances explore,
And find, perchance, some realm more blest,
Some isle of beauty and of rest
In the far regions of the WEST—
Such visions floated in the sight
Of daring spirits ere the light
Of science shed its radiance bright;
And Madog, stedfast still to shun
The height which safe he might have won,
(For, still the idol and the stand
Of Gwynedd, but to wave his hand
Had been the signal to restore
His rights resigned and sovereign power),
Recalling oft the mystic strain
That wildly burst from Meurig Hên,
And broke his heart and scared his brain,

Resolved to tempt the watery way
Where sets the god-like star of day.

His parting beams were tipping now
The spangled juts of Wyddfa's[76] brow,
As in the vision's utmost bound,
The mountain pyramid he crowned,
That, shelving up from Arfon's shore,
On Meirion frowns across Traeth Mawr.
Seemed the great ruler of the sky
To veil before such majesty,
And touched his stern and awful peak
As smiling maid a giant's cheek ;
While his long intermediate rays
O'er landscape blush—on ocean blaze,
And cheer with a benignant smile
That gentle martyr's[77] holy isle.
Who in the dread attempt to save
Her sire could heathen outrage brave,
And so illustrate in her death
Both filial love and Christian faith.

---

[76] Snowdon.

[77] St. Tudval, a daughter of Brychan Brycheiniog, King of South Wales, martyred by Picts and Saxons, fifth century. The island alluded to in Cardigan Bay as well as a large town in Glamorganshire commemorate this British martyr.

But more than islet, rock, or wave,
  Majestic mount or storied grove,
That sun-light rested on the brave,
  Inspiring and responding love.

Along the margin of the flood,
  On every headland, point, and height,
Dense living masses lingering stood,
  Who did in heart and soul unite.

One anxious way strained every neck,
  Clung every heart and every eye
Upon the still receding speck,
  Until it melted into sky.

And still above the plashing oar,
  The sighing wind and rippling sea,
Was wafted from the peopled shore,
  A nation's mourning melody :

" Farewell, our brave defender,
  Honour, praise, and love to thee
With heart and voice we render—
  Waft thee heaven across the sea !

" Thy pathless way before thee
  Leads o'er the treach'rous wave,

The heavens glitter o'er thee,
    But where shall be thy grave?

"Arthur[78] slumbers in Llyn Tegid—
    O'er the giant Gwallog[79] weeps
Gentle Carrog—Urien Rheged[80]
    'Neath the holy Island sleeps—

"But when Glory's sad emotion
    Mourns her hero Madog dead,
Over all the world-wide ocean
    Must her world-wide tears be shed!"

The shallop lightly skimmed
    Across the glinting sea—
Its snowy sails were trimmed,
    Its dancing step was free.

Who would have thought that dark
    And sad a heart could be
Within that fairy bark,
    Upon that sparkling sea!

---

[78] See note 55, p. 96.

[79] Gwallog, a British hero of gigantic stature and surpassing beauty, lies buried by the river Carrog, County Carnarvon, near the village of Llanwnda.

[80] A pre-eminent hero in early British history, who, after performing prodigies of valour, fell at the siege of Lindisfarne by the hand of Ida, a Saxon King.

Yet on that gilded deck
    There was a manly heart.
And it was nigh to break
    From that loved shore to part.

And from that heart's excess[81]
    Out spoke the tuneful tongue,
And thus did it express
    The grief its core that wrung—

PRINCE MADOG'S FAREWELL.
(BY MRS. HEMANS.[82])

"Why lingers my gaze where the last hues of day
    On the hills of my country in loveliness sleep?—
Too fair is the sight for a wanderer whose way
    Lies far o'er the measureless wilds of the deep—
Fall, shadows of evening, and veil the green shore,
That the heart of the mighty may waver no more.

---

[81] "Out of the abundance of the heart the mouth speaketh."—Luke chap. vi. 45.

[82] I have taken the liberty of closing with a reprint of this spirited and too little known piece, by the most charming of England's poetesses, which was written to the arrangement of a favourite Welsh melody by the late talented harpist, Mr John Parry, the father of the present master of that name now of such world-wide fame.

Why rise on my thoughts, ye free songs of the land,
   Where the harp's lofty soul on each wild wind is borne?
Be hushed—be forgotten—for ne'er shall the hand
   Of the minstrel with melody greet my return;
Ah, no—let your echoes still float on the breeze,
And my heart shall be strong for the conquest of seas.

It is not for the land of our sires to give birth
   To bosoms that shrink when their trial is nigh.
Away—we shall bear over ocean and earth
   A name and a spirit that never can die—
My course to the winds, to the waves I resign,
But my soul's quenchless fire, O my country, is THINE!"

A PRINCE OF WALES

LONG AGO.

Appendix.

A PRINCE OF WALES
LONG AGO.

Appendix.

NOTE A.

"Land of the lovely, the brave, and the free!"
Page 5.

OF the native valour of the Ancient Britons all the records of history bear abundant testimony. Their efforts to maintain independence against the Roman legions are mentioned by the Roman Historians with more of honour than they condescended to bestow upon any other of the nations of the then known world subjected to their arms — such being the inevitable fate attending the contest between skill and discipline, on the one hand, and native courage, unaided by those indispensable qualities, on the other.

After this conquest the armies of Rome were recruited, and its failing strength long sustained by the stalwart

British youth, as pourtrayed, with entire truthfulness, in Sir Walter Scott's historical novel "Count Robert of Paris," and although five centuries of subjection had left them, at the close of the Roman dominion, unable, for the moment, to resort to their long unused weapons, they yet speedily resumed in the fastnesses of those mountains, which have since been their home, the indestructible spirit of independence, and the courage necessary to sustain it.

The interval which separates those days from our own is sufficiently marked, in every era, with manifestations of this Aboriginal British spirit, of which such scenes as this tale attempts to recal present instances.

At the moment of committing these pages to the press the nation has been for some days in an agony of suspense to receive from the East the details of the victorious struggle, of which the lightning speed of the telegraph has only communicated the general results. But although a few sentences only are all that the country has yet received of a contest in which thousands of the British force have yielded up their lives, *two* of those sentences are devoted to the Regiment known in the service as "The Welsh Fusileers."

"The 23rd Regiment lost all its officers but three,
"of whom Captain Bell was the senior."

"Already it is known that the light division has
"suffered most severely in this action, and especially
"the 23rd Fusileers, who have renewed on the banks
"of the Alma that heroic gallantry which they displayed
"of old on the fields of Egypt, the Peninsula, and
"Flanders."

Such, too, is the just meed of honour given forth by the world-speaking voice of the great journal of Europe.

While the standards of the Regiment will bear through future struggles these records of its valour, their fellow-countrymen, we trust, will long have to recognise that, at home, the Ancient British are as obedient to the laws of their country as they are ready abroad to lay down their lives for its honour and renown. In the Principality, such is the security and confidence in public order, that there does not exist a barrack for soldiers, and twice every year the Judges, on their circuits, repeat at each town they visit their testimony to the total or comparative absence of offences against the laws.

Appendix.

Note B.

"Within the Celtic line, some bow-shot length,
A structure stood."
Page 8.

"Madog his fortress court maintains,
Which still his honoured name retains,
To guard, as erst, the frontier plains."
Page 76.

PLAS MADOC, the opening scene of this tale of the ancient time, still stands on an elevation, a short distance from the village of Ruabon, in a position well calculated for a frontier residence of the ancient lords of Cambria. It is, perhaps, one of the oldest mansions in the Principality, and is associated in tradition with the still more interesting structure of Dinäs Bran, of which the ruins yet frown, in majestic desolation, over the well-known village of Llangollen, and the abbey ruins of Valle Crucis and monumental pillar of Eliseg, to which Antiquaries, with sufficient authority, assign the date of the 7th century.

APPENDIX.

These visible landmarks of the olden time are more deserving of being noted and preserved in the Principality than elsewhere, because the customs of the British having prohibited written records of the events which in their time swept over these beautiful scenes, and agitated human affairs in a degree unknown to the more placid current which marks the period of written history, have left no other record by which our imagination can fill up the living picture of the past.

Very slight and shadowy are the traditions which yet hover over this border district. Plâs Madoc, as has been stated, is said to have been a Royal residence; the lands around it, and lying between the mansion and the high road, near which also the railway now passes, are supposed to have been the scene of some of the most sanguinary conflicts of the border, for it is close to Plâs Madoc, and through its grounds, that the frontier boundary, still to be plainly seen for many a mile of its course, and yet known as "Offa's Dyke," presents its speechless but significant elevation.

The very name of the parish tells its history as a border district; for the name *Ruabon*, derived from *Rhud*, red, and *Avon*, river, is supposed to denote the sanguinary stains which the river, now pouring its peaceful stream through the village, received when friend and foe, Roman, Saxon, Briton, or Norman, in indiscriminate slaughter, mingled with its waters. The river is known by the name of *Afon-Goch*, another term for red, and as it winds around the foot of the Gardden hill, a very remarkable British fortified camp near the village, it vividly realizes the beautiful lines which Sir Walter Scott addressed to another stream, certainly not better entitled to national associations:—

> " Sweet Teviot! on thy silver tide
>   The glaring bale-fires blaze no more,
> No longer steel-clad warriors ride
>   Along thy wild and willow'd shore,
> Where'er thou wind'st, by dale or hill,
> All, all is peaceful, all is still,
>   As if thy waves, since Time was born,
> Since first they rolled upon the Tweed,
> Had only heard the shepherd's reed,
>   Nor started at the bugle-horn.
>
> " Unlike the tide of human time
>   Which, though it change in ceaseless flow,
> Retains each grief, retains each crime
>   Its earliest course was doomed to know:
> And darker as it downward bears
> Is stained with past and present tears."
>
> LAY OF THE LAST MINSTREL.
Canto IV.

The district is remarkable for features of interest of a varying and striking character.

APPENDIX.

The Aqueduct which carries the waters of the canal across the gorge of the Vale of Llangollen, though at one time a marvel of engineering skill, has recently been surpassed by the viaduct thrown across the same vale for the passage of the railway.

The magnificent domain of Wynnstay immediately fronts the scene selected for the opening of the tale, and the site of the mansion may be considered to form the Saxon boundary of the neutral ground, of which Plâs Madoc forms the British boundary.

In the distance stands pre-eminent over the landscape Chirk Castle, keeping watch and ward, as it were, over the district, and it is undoubtedly one of the finest specimens of a feudal mansion to be found in the kingdom.

On various elevations may be seen, marking the boundaries of rival estates, or squirearchies, towers still representing, on a small scale, the belligerent associations of the district, while over all frowns in stately isolation the mountain peak of Dinäs Bran, one of the most ancient and best preserved remains of British castellated defences in North Wales.

Appendix.

Note C.

> " For, know all we of modern days,
>   Who boast of liberty and laws,
>   Our British fathers share the praise—
>   They edged the sword that freedom draws.
>
> " And though it rusted long beneath
>   Unblest dominion, feudal strife;
>   It burst, in time, the crumbling sheath,
>   And, flaming, guards that tree of life."
>
> Page 64

THE Laws, Manners, and Customs of the BRITISH RACE have never lost their hold upon the curiosity, or even the sympathies of the English. But the extent to which their claims to be considered as the basis, the very root and origin, of the existing jurisprudence of the Commonwealth of this Empire have been overlooked, ignored, and even vehemently contradicted by English writers on such subjects, in all the ages subsequent to Saxon rule in this island, is very remarkable. It indicates a jealousy, on the part of those who have held the pen of history and the sword of Government, strikingly characteristic of what we discover by other signs, namely, a settled system to obliterate from the recollection of the masses of the population those ancient, indigenous laws, manners, and customs, which springing from the very hearts of the people themselves, have here, as in all other countries of which the early history is known to us, been ever the strongest and most lasting bulwarks against the encroachments of arbitrary power, injustice, and usurpation.

In this point of view, the unanimous concurrence of Saxon writers in early times, in refusing to do justice to the ancient laws and institutions of those amongst whom they came to hold sway, must be classed amongst the other devices to which recourse was had to extinguish the national spirit of the British; and the strong measures by which the Bards were exterminated or silenced, on the one hand, and the unparalleled strength with which those strongholds were required to be constructed, whereby the Saxons and Normans sought to maintain their position against the still independent tribes of Cambria, are noble testimonials of the native vigour, the all but indomitable tenacity, with which Britons of the old time maintained their rights.

In the present day it would not detract from, but would

ennoble, the entire national history of our Empire, to identify this Ancient British Race, our veritable forefathers, with those struggles for liberty at home and power abroad, by which the story of our now common country sheds its light over the world.

Were it not out of place to append to a light tale of poesy the weighty archæology that such a topic involves, it would be a very gratifying task, and not by any means so difficult as might be imagined, to remove the huge masses of Saxon Codes, Norman Edicts, and Parliamentary Statutes, under which the ancient laws of Britain have lain hid for ages, and to disclose, in the Songs of the Bards—the legends and customs of the people, and their still surviving institutions, (of which the Eisteddfod is a remarkable example) — the spirit of the laws; in some instances, the very forms of administration, and, in almost every particular, the roots of all that is valuable, all that has figured most honourably in our Juridical, and even our Political History; and it may further be permitted to hazard the suggestion, that, if such an investigation were fairly entered upon, and any seeds of these ancient, aboriginal times should be found to have lain dormant, such grains of ancient growth may yet be found to retain fructifying powers in them, just as the particles of corn that fall from the swathes of the exhumed Egyptians are said still to manifest vegetative life.

Those who may desire to enter upon such inquiry, or who may regard this suggestion as too much savouring of that faculty whose proper sphere is poetry, will do well to consult the "Commentary" of Sir Francis Palgrave, on the English Commonwealth ; and, perhaps, a short extract or two from that admirable work may be necessary to justify the intrusion of such a topic on the general reader.

In his Preface, Sir Francis observes, " Political events " generally occupy the first station in the pages of the " Historian ; political institutions the second : judicial " policy and jurisprudence the third and last : *but the* " *character of a people mainly depends upon their laws.*"

Then, what does this truly constitutional authority say of the laws of Ancient Britain ?

" It is more important to remark, that the character of " the British legislation is enhanced by comparison with " the laws which were put in practice by the other nations " of the middle ages. The indignant pride of the Britons, " who despised their implacable enemies the Anglo-Saxons " as a race of rude barbarians, whose touch was impurity, " will not be considered as any decisive test of superior

"civilization. But the triads of the laws of Hoel Dda
" exceed the Anglo-Saxon and other Teutonic custumals
" in the same manner as the Elegies of Lewarch Hên,
" and the Odes of Taliessin soar above the Ballads of the
" Edda. Law had become a science amongst the Britons,
" and its volumes exhibit the jurisprudence of a rude
" nation, shaped and modelled by thinking men, and which
" had derived both stability and equity from the labours
" of its expounders."—*Page* 37.

In a previous page (35) he states the well known fact, that " so long as the Druids were the sole depositaries " of British jurisprudence, the law was oral and tradi- " tionary. Their doctrines were recorded in verse, and " the faint echoes of the Bardic strains can yet be dis- " covered in the triads of Dyvnwal Moelmud, who, before " the crown and sceptre of London were wrested by the " Saxons, reigned over the Island."

Faint, indeed, were the echoes of the Bardic strains, because each succeeding oppressor, whether foreign or domestic, found safety alone in the degree in which these strains, together with the Bards themselves, could be silenced and exterminated. But, happily for the liberties of this country, these strains preserved an undying echo in the feelings and affections of the people; and though the Saxons. within a few years after their settlement in the Island, collected the laws, and, putting them into writing, assumed to themselves, and gave to their codes, a Saxon name, yet, in fact, these codes, renewed from reign to reign during the Saxon rule, and forced in some form or other upon the acceptance of each Norman from William the First to the last of his race,—kept sacredly in mind through the troubled times of the Tudors. ratified in the blood and expulsion of the Stuarts,—are still the basis of the jurisprudence of the British Empire, in spirit and sense, though the forms and the names may have long since been forgotten.

Sir Francis Palgrave bears direct testimony to the similarity between the British and the Anglo-Saxon codes; and. after enumerating the particulars in which they so agree, including, "perhaps, the constitution of the tribunals " which were founded upon that division," he adds, " these " being the chief features of the law, and its administration, " the question, whether such analogous customs be of " British or of Saxon origin, is little more than a mere " verbal dispute, very difficult to decide, and perfectly " useless when decided."

It is proposed to offer one more extract, whereby it will appear clearly, that such laws were of British, and not of Saxon origin, first taking leave to differ, with great deference to Sir Francis Palgrave, from his opinion, that such question is " perfectly useless." for if our Commonwealth, be superior as it is our duty and pride to believe it still to be to all others—worthy to be the model for the vast communities that derive from us their name and history — surely, it constitutes an additional claim to the veneration of ourselves, and of those future nations, our children, that this Commonwealth is, in fact, the same that was handed down from unknown antiquity, in the " verses of the Druids," and " being shaped and modelled " by thinking men," were, even in those times, as superior to the laws of other nations as the " Odes of Taliessin " soared above the Ballads of the Edda."

It is in the fifteenth chapter of his work that Sir Francis Palgrave clearly proves that the amalgamation between the Saxons and the Ancient Britons was effected — in a great degree by mutual arrangement — from which that portion of the ancient people who occupied the district now known as North Wales refused, as it were, to be parties, maintaining still their separate language, laws, and customs. Thus we find that, although the Ancient Britons never condescended to resort to the pen to preserve the true history of their alliance with the Saxon, but gave to the Chroniclers of their enemies their national character, as well as their laws; yet we find, that at a Witenagemote, or National Council, convened by Athelstane, no other laymen but British Sub-Reguli were allowed to be present, such council being assembled by the Sovereign as the "Ruler of the Britons." And, while the western shires were almost entirely composed of Britons, they so far recognised, voluntarily, the expediency of the Saxon Government as to aid, on many occasions, under their native princes, in extending the Saxon rule.

That the Saxon chronicles in which the history of these times is alone recorded, should have represented the Britons as being subdued and suppressed by the Saxons, instead of the Saxons as being tolerated and permitted to make themselves useful to the Britons, calls to mind the analogous portrait of the lion whose history, as recorded by the sculptor, presented an unconditional subjection to the superior prowess of man. As the lion when contemplating this exhibition suggested, that had the artist been a lion the position of the parties would probably have been reversed, so those who may feel an interest in deepening the foundations of the British character and institutions may fairly regard the ancient Britons as being, in this respect, the original type of the historical British Lion contemplating his portrait by Saxon artists.

"All these facts," observes Sir Francis, will afford "much matter for reflection, and convince us of the "great difficulty of penetrating into the real history of "nations. Read the Chroniclers, and it will appear as "if the Britons had been entirely overwhelmed by the "influx of the Teutonic population; and it is only by "minute and painful inquiry that we ascertain the exist- "ence of the subjugated races, concealed amidst the "invaders."

If the views of Sir Francis Palgrave as expressed in the first extract given in this Appendix be correct, an inquiry sufficient to establish an identity in the leading principles of our existing Constitution — that Constitution which is said to be the admiration of the world — with the Constitution of the Ancient Britons, needs not to be very painful or minute. Sir Francis truly states, that "the character of a people depends upon their laws;" and "it is utterly impossible to obtain a correct view of the "general administration of the state unless we fully under- "stand the spirit of the institutions which pervade the "the community, and regulate the daily actings and doings "of mankind."

Any one who has had the curiosity to enter the Courts of Common Law, at Westminster, will have been impressed with the gravity and true dignity which their course of proceedings exhibits; and it ought not to detract from the reverence which the spectacle is calculated to inspire, that those unimpeachable administrators of the laws and customs of England are there ranged, side by side, four in each Court, bound by their oath of office to administer the law on the very same principles as the law was administered amongst the Ancient Britons, from the earliest period of which the faintest trace is left to us. The Laws of the Druids were not more " oral and traditionary " than the Common Law, at this day, administered at Westminster; and when it is also borne in mind — what all our legal writers inform us — that this is a peculiarity which distinguishes the English Courts of Justice and Jurisprudence from almost all other known systems; that it is this very peculiarity which the people of this country have on frequent occasions in their history defended from encroachment, with the utmost energy and determination; it is not claiming more than the Ancient Britons are entitled to, nor more than it is the interest of our national character to concede, that those very grave and reverend seigniors, the Lords Chief Justices of the Courts of Common Law and their colleagues on the bench are, in truth, the veritable successors of the Lawgivers — for such, in fact, they are at this hour, as in the days of the Druids — in unbroken succession from our ancestors, the aboriginal inhabitants of Britain.

ERRATA.

In page 11, line 14, for "whom," read "who."
,, 15. ,, 18. omit period at " orbs."
,, 28, ,, 20, omit comma at "bounds,"
,, 40, ,, 5, for "their," read "the."
,, 44, ,, 11, for "reverend," read "reverent."
,, 62, ,, 7, for "mead," read "meed."
,, 76. .. 14. for "Uther." read "Uthyr."
,, 79, ,, 15, for "surphureous," read "sulphureous."
,, 87, ,, 18, for "enwrapped," read "enrapt."
,, 92, ,, 18, for "On," read "To," for "hung," "clung."

CPSIA information can be obtained
at www.ICGtesting.com
Printed in the USA
BVHW042348070221
599595BV00030B/459